Spreadsheet Projects

in Excel for Advanced Level

Julian Mott and Ian Rendell

Hodder & Stoughton

A MEMBER OF THE HODDER HEADLINE GROUP

Acknowledgements

The authors would like to thank the following people who have helped in the writing of this book: Sam Hill, Nicola Joiner, Jane Mott, Lucy Mott, Paul Reed, Helen Royall, Andrew Smith.

Orders: please contact Bookpoint Ltd, 130 Milton Park, Abingdon, Oxon OX14 4SB. Telephone: (44) 01235 827720, Fax: (44) 1235 400454. Lines are open from 9.00 – 6.00, Monday to Saturday, with a 24 hour message answering service. Email address: orders@bookpoint.co.uk

British Library Cataloguing in Publication Data

A catalogue record for this title is available from The British Library

ISBN 0 340 8 0007 0

First published 2001
Impression number   10 9 8 7 6 5 4 3
Year   2005 2004 2003 2002

Typeset by Multiplex Techniques, Orpington
Printed in Great Britain for Hodder & Stoughton Education, a division of Hodder Headline Plc, 338 Euston Road, London NW1 3BH by Martins the Printers, Berwick-upon-Tweed.

Contents

Introduction

■ Aims

The book is aimed primarily at students studying the A/S and A levels in ICT offered by AQA, OCR and Edexcel. The book offers advice and support materials for the practical component of the specification, making candidates aware of analysing, designing, implementing, testing and evaluating solutions to problems using the advanced features of a software package.

The book could also prove useful, however, for students studying A/S and A levels in Computing where a software package solution to an ICT system can be offered as an alternative approach to a programming solution.

The materials and approach used in the book might also be applicable to students on many courses in further and higher education where a study of spreadsheets through Microsoft Excel is necessary.

■ What are the advanced features

Excel ?

The following advice is intended only for guidance. Teachers should use this in conjunction with the Specification and Examiners Reports to ensure the correct features are being used appropriately.

Use of these features alone does not guarantee high marks. It is down to how the student uses some of them to solve and document an ICT problem. Students might use the following as a reference document to ensure their work takes into account some of the features available.

Students are expected to make use of features beyond the simple arithmetic of $+$, $-$, $\times$, $\div$ and simple formulae.

Solutions might include linked sheets and not a series of unrelated 'flat' sheets. Where appropriate cells and cell ranges should be named to improve readability and aid development.

Students should be introduced to some of the mathematical and financial functions available in Excel. Functions such as IF and LOOKUP would certainly and routinely have a high priority.

Dialog boxes, combo boxes, drop down lists and UserForms are ways of aiding and automating input that students might be introduced to.

Pivot tables and multiple scenarios are other advanced features and are equally appropriate at this level.

Students would be expected to use macros to automate commonly used features and sort and process data appropriately.

Programming and the use of Visual Basic are not usually within the spirit of the specifications or the systems promoted in this book. The chosen software package should drive the solution and not Visual Basic code. However students might tinker with the code it to enhance their solution.

Students are expected to work towards the production of fully automated and customised solutions thereby hiding the software from the user. Customising menus and interfaces, removing toolbars and automating features are some of the options available that students should include.

Excel 97/2000 issues

Excel 2000 offers a number of new features which are clearly listed under Microsoft Help but all the materials in this book work in both Excel 2000 and Excel 97.

Office 2000 now uses intelligent menu technology which means your most commonly used commands from each menu are moved to the top of the list. This can be irritating if you are new to the later version. You might like to remove this feature: see Turning on and off 'Intelligent' Menus, page 192.

How to use this book

The book assumes students have a working knowledge of Windows and Windows-based software. Students will have been introduced to spreadsheets via the National Curriculum or the study of ICT at Key Stages 3 and 4.

The book can be used as a formal teaching aid by lecturers or students can work independently through the self-study units in class or away from the classroom.

Part One takes the student through a series of self-study units which demonstrate the higher level features of Excel, together with exercises using these features. These can be worked through as stand-alone units but initially are probably best worked through in sequence.

Part Two takes the student through the implementation of a system using a range of Excel features. The system is fictitious and has been designed to incorporate as many features as is possible for demonstration purposes only. This part pulls together and builds on much of the work covered in Part One.

Part Three covers the major issues in documenting coursework projects and offers pointers, hints and examples of good practice.

Part Four offers a range of useful tips to support the chapters and should provide interesting reading. These could be used as further activities for students. It is hoped that they can be the starting point for finding out even more about Excel.

A note to students and lecturers

It is important to note that the system used in the text is not being put forward for a particular grade at any level. The system is fictitious and is aimed at showing the student the potential of Microsoft Excel and how software features can be incorporated to produce a working ICT system.

All boards provide exemplar materials, support and training, and it is vital that students in conjunction with their tutors are guided by the specifications.

The documentation of ICT solutions at this level follows the systems life-cycle approach of analysis, design, implementation, testing and evaluation. Again, though, different specifications and different solutions will have a different emphasis.

A word of real caution. Students must on no account copy materials in text books and submit them for examination. Moderators, examiners and the exam boards are very aware of published exemplar materials. You will be penalised severely.

■ Choosing a coursework project

Don't try to do everything.

Using every single feature of Excel would almost certainly lead to a very contrived project. It is better to choose a problem, which involves some of the advanced features rather than all of them in the solution.

Don't try to do too much.

It is easy to be over-ambitious. Computerising the payroll, income tax, national insurance and pension records of a county council or producing a stock control system for a multinational company is unrealistic at this level. It is best to stick to something that you know you can achieve.

Don't try to do too little.

However the opposite is also true. Your project must not be too simple at this level. It should go beyond simple arithmetic. If you can set the system up in a few lessons, it is likely that the project chosen will not have enough scope.

Do try to find a real user.

It is best to choose a real problem with a real end-user. The user could be one of your parents or a friend or neighbour. They could be a member of staff in your school or college. Having a real user does make analysis, testing and evaluating your solution all the easier. For some courses, a real end-user is essential.

■ Ideas for projects

Task	Input data	Processing requirements	Output information
1. Car insurance premium calculator	Details of the car. Personal details of the driver, e.g. age and gender, their postcode and the number of years' no-claims bonus.	Look up insurance group of car from a table. Look up costs of insurance for that group from a table. Calculate costs. Calculate discounts. Store the information for possible later use.	The cost of insurance. Printed quotation with the date for future reference.
2. Personal computer price calculator	Details of the chosen computer (which could also be chosen from a list) such as processor speed, size of RAM, hard disk capacity, video card, monitor and modem.	Look up the price of components from a table. Calculate the cost of the PC. Details of the price and the name of the potential buyer will be stored for possible later use.	The cost of the computer including a printed quotation.
3. Sports league table	Teams in the league. The scores of the matches in the league played so far. Possibly dates of matches.	Calculate the result of each match and therefore the number of points gained and goal difference for each team. This information will be put into a league table and sorted into order.	The league table. A full table of results. This might also include printed output, depending on the requirements of the user.
4. Carpet cost calculator	Dimensions of room(s). Requirements (heavy duty, light use, etc.). Material costs. Prices.	Look up prices in a table. Calculate costs of carpet. Add on costs of fitting, VAT, etc.	A printed invoice with full breakdown of costs. Scenarios could be set up of typical rooms in houses.

Task	Input data	Processing requirements	Output information
5. **Invoice production for a small printing company**	Customer details. Work done. Number of documents printed. Size of documents. Type of paper used. The number of photographs included, etc.	Look up the price of different items from a table. Calculate the cost of the order. Store the information so that a record can be kept of payment.	An on-screen account and a printed invoice Scenarios could be set up of typical print runs.
6. **Heating costs calculator**	The dimensions of a house. The number of rooms and the type of windows. Existence of cavity wall and loft insulation. The required temperature.	Look up information in a table. Calculate how much it will cost to heat a house for a year. Store the information for future comparisons.	The likely number of units used. The cost of heating. Scenarios could be set up of typical types of houses.
7. **Department accounts**	Starting balance. Details of items ordered. Possible future purchases.	Calculate running total of the balance. Predict likely year-end figures. Calculate carried forward totals	Current and predicted financial position day-by-day, possibly also in the form of a graph.
8. **Foreign exchange calculator**	Country to be visited (chosen from a list). Present currency (chosen from a list). The amount of currency required.	Look up currency rates in a table. Calculate what you will get and what it will cost.	Exact cost. Amount provided. Exchange rate including a printed version.

Task	Input data	Processing requirements	Output information
9. **Billing system (e.g. gas bills)**	Customer names and addresses. Amount of gas used in the last quarter. Details of new customers.	Looks up customer details in a table. Calculates total bill including standing charge and VAT.	Automatically prints out bills. Prints an analysis of gas usage. Scenarios could be set up of typical bills.
10. **Golf scoreboard**	Details of each player's score on each hole over a championship. Details of the course and par for each hole.	Calculate each player's score. Calculate current position compared with par. Sort the scores into order.	Print sorted details of total scores. Display leaderboard for current leading players.
11. **Stocks and shares portfolio**	Details of share portfolio. Latest share prices.	Keep an up-to-date record of the value of shareholding. Calculate the profit and percentage profit made on each investment.	Provide up-to-date information about shares, possibly in graphical form.
12. **Dietary analysis calculator**	The age and gender of the person would need to be entered as this affects the recommended daily intake. Details of your daily diet including quantities of each food stuff.	Look up the food information from a table. Calculating the intake of calories, protein, fibre, fat, etc and compare with the recommended daily intake for someone of that age and gender. Information on different patients may be stored for comparison purposes.	Report on daily intake and how this compares with their recommended daily intake. This information can be presented in the form of a graph.
13. **Car price calculator**	Details of the chosen car and accessories such as alloy wheels, metallic paint, CD interchanger, etc.	Look up the price of accessories from a table. Calculate the cost of the car. Details of the price and the name of the potential buyer will be stored for possible later use.	The cost of the car including a printed quotation.

Task	Input data	Processing requirements	Output information
14. Electronic attendance register	Student names.	Calculate total attendance figures.	Print details of attendance.
	Attendance details.	Calculate average attendance figures.	Print attendance statistics and graphs.
	Records of notes received.	Sort details into order of worst attendance.	Produce lists of those for whom no note has been received.
15. Electronic mark book	Student names.	Calculate average marks.	Print out full student records.
	Student marks for various assignments, homeworks and tests.	Compare individual results with the class average.	Print out predicted grades.
		Aggregate marks.	Print out student report based on marks in the markbook.
		Predict grades.	
16. The fast food restaurant till and stock controller	The types of meal purchased (selected from a list or by a macro button).	Calculate the cost of a meal.	Tell the customer the cost of the meal.
		Keep a record of sales for stock control purposes.	Provide stock ordering information in printed form for the staff.

Project timetable

A project timetable helps you ensure that the work-load is spread evenly throughout the project period, allowing for other factors such as module tests in ICT and other subjects, holidays and half-terms, work-loads in other subjects, etc.

You should break your project up into sub-tasks and draw up the timetable at the start and try to stick to it. If you don't you can end up with too much to do at the last minute. This means that deadlines cannot be met and the final sections are rushed and only get low marks.

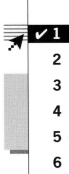

Introduction to Excel

In this chapter you will revise and review the basic spreadsheet features in Microsoft Excel such as:

- the general spreadsheet layout of rows, columns and cells;
- entering data into a spreadsheet;
- different data types such as currency, text, numbers and percentages;
- inserting and deleting rows and columns;
- highlighting cells and cell ranges;
- the general formatting of data, different fonts, font sizes and alignments;
- entering simple formulas to carry out calculations;
- the Windows environment and the Excel Standard and Formatting toolbars;
- using copy and paste to speed up the entry of data and formulas;
- saving and printing work.

If you are very familiar with these features, you may want to miss out Examples 1 and 3 and only do Example 2 and The School Play.

Worked example 1 is a very simple, basic costing spreadsheet covering most of the above features. The student is given a step-by-step guide.

Worked example 2 is a small problem involving naming cells and absolute references.

Worked example 3 is a real problem investigating the profits from a school vending machine. It covers all the above skills. The student is encouraged to move at a faster pace.

The School Play is a more complex task using the above skills but you are on your own!

▶ WORKED EXAMPLE 1:   A simple costing spreadsheet

■ Entering the data

1. Click on cell A1. Enter **Customer Name**. The text is too long to fit in the cell, so click on **Format, Cells.** Click on the **Alignment** tab and click on **Wrap text**. The text will be displayed on multiple lines.

	A	B	C	D	E	F	G
1	Customer Name	Charge per hour	Hours worked	Cost of labour	Cost of materials	Call out charge	Total bill
2	Trescothick	12	2		4	10	
3	Derrick	12	3		18	10	
4	Allen	12	4		40	10	
5	Crowe	12	1		15	15	
6	George	12	2		12	15	
7						Daily total	

Hint:

■ If you have formatted a cell to currency and you wish to convert it back to number format, click on the **Comma Style** icon.

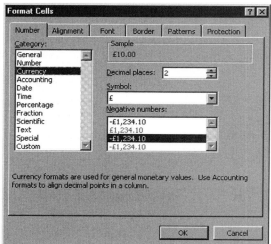

2. Enter the other column headings as shown.

3. Enter the data into column A as shown. Some of the names do not quite fit in the cells. When you have finished entering the names, click on the **A** column heading and click on **Format, Column, AutoFit Selection**

4. Enter the rest of the data as shown above. You will notice that text goes to the left of a cell and numbers to the right.

5. Click on column heading **A** and from the menu click on **Insert, Columns.**

6. Click on row heading **1** and from the menu choose **Insert, Rows.**

7. Highlight cells C3 to C7 by dragging with the mouse and click on the **Currency** icon.

8. Highlight cells F3 to G7 and click on the **Currency** icon.

9. Highlight row 2 and click on the **Center** icon and the **Bold** text icon.

10. Highlight cells G8 and click on the **Center** icon and the **Bold** text icon.

Many of these formatting operations can just as easily be carried out by highlighting the cell or cell range and right clicking the mouse.

This brings up the above menu above left. Clicking on **Format, Cells** displays the Format Cells options.

Highlight some data in a cell and experiment with the options available

Entering the formulas

11. Click on cell E3 and enter the formula `=C3*D3`

12. The formula in H3 is the sum of E3, F3 and G3. Click on H3, type `=E3+F3+G3` or `=SUM(E3:G3)`

13. We now use copy and paste to enter the formula down the column. Click on E3 and click the **Copy** icon, a flashing grid should appear. Highlight cells E4 to E7 and click on the **Paste** icon.

14. Use the same method to copy the formula in H3 into the cells H4 to H7.

15. To finish off the spreadsheet we need to sum column H and put the answer in H8. In H8 enter `=SUM(H3:H7)` or highlight the cells H3 to H8 and click on the **AutoSum** icon.

16. Your finished spreadsheet should look like the one shown on the right.
Save your file as **Bill.xls**

	A	B	C	D	E	F	G	H
1								
2		Customer name	Charge per hour	Hours worked	Cost of labour	Cost of materials	Call out charge	Total bill
3		Trescothick	£ 12.00	2	£24.00	£ 4.00	£ 10.00	£38.00
4		Derrick	£ 12.00	3	£36.00	£ 18.00	£ 10.00	£64.00
5		Allen	£ 12.00	4	£48.00	£ 40.00	£ 10.00	£98.00
6		Crowe	£ 12.00	1	£12.00	£ 15.00	£ 15.00	£42.00
7		George	£ 12.00	2	£24.00	£ 12.00	£ 15.00	£51.00
8							Daily total	£293.00

WORKED EXAMPLE 2: Mileage calculator

A motorist buying a new car wants to know how much it will cost to run in a year. One of the major costs is the cost of fuel and she wants to investigate how much she might spend on petrol each year.

	A	B	C	D	E
1	37	mpg			price/litre
2					
3	miles	gallons	litres	cost	
4	1000				
5	2000				
6	3000				
7	4000				
8	5000				
9	6000				
10	7000				
11	8000				
12	9000				
13	10000				
14	11000				
15	12000				

1. Set out the spreadsheet as on the right.

2. In cell B4 enter the formula =A4/A1 . This will work out how many gallons of petrol are needed to drive 1000 miles.

If you copy the formula in B4 down to B15, it does not work. Try it and see. The computer has changed the reference to =A5/A2 , =A6/A3 , which will not work.

This is because we want the formula to keep the reference to A1, e.g. =A5/A1 =A6/A1 etc.

There are two ways in which we can put this right.

(a) Absolute references

An absolute reference is one that does not change when it is copied. It is shown by using the $ sign, e.g. A1.

3. In cell B4 enter the formula =A4/A1 The reference to A4 will change as this cell is copied but the reference to A1 will not change.

4. Copy this cell into all the cells down to B15.

(b) Naming cells

We can give a cell a name and use this name in formulas. Naming cells is good practice.

5. Click on cell A1. Click on **Insert, Name, Define**. Call the cell **mpg**.

> **Hint:**
> ■ Use the Drag Copy Short Cut to set up cells A4 to A15.
> (See page 175)

6. In cell B4 enter the formula =A4/mpg Copy this cell into all the cells down to B15.

Complete the spreadsheet as follows:

7. There are 4.54 litres in a gallon. In cell C4 enter the formula =B4*4.54

8. Copy this cell into all the cells down to C15.

9. In cell D1 enter the price of a litre of petrol. (Remember you will need to format this cell to currency.)

10. Click on cell D1 again. Click on **Insert, Name, Define**. Call the cell **price**.

11. In cell D4 enter the formula **=C4*price**

12. Format this cell to currency and copy it into all the cells down to D15.

Save your file as **Mileage.xls**

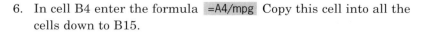

▶ WORKED EXAMPLE 3: The vending machine

Hint:
■ Use copy and paste.

You are going to set up a spreadsheet to look at the profits made by the vending machines in a school.

1. Enter the data as shown below. Enter 10 for the cans sold. Spreadsheets are often set up with easy numbers so the model can be checked easily.

	A	B	C	D	E	F	G	H	I	J	K
		Mon	Tues	Wed	Thurs	Fri	Total sales	Cost price	Sell price	Profit per can	Total profit
2	Cola	10	10	10	10	10					
3	Diet Cola	10	10	10	10	10					
4	Sunkist	10	10	10	10	10					
5	Lilt	10	10	10	10	10					
6	Cherry Cola	10	10	10	10	10					
7	Total cans sold									Weekly profit	

Entering the data:

2. The school buys the cans of drink at 15p. Enter the cost prices in column H. Remember to enter the prices as 0.15 and copy and paste (replicate) is a quick way of completing the column. Format to currency.

3. The school sells the cans of drink at 65p. Enter the selling price in column I and format to currency.

Setting up the formulas

4. The total sales of cola are calculated by adding the sales from Mon to Fri. In cell G2 enter the formula `=SUM(B2:F2)` Complete column G.

5. The profit per can is calculated by taking the cost price from the sell price. In cell J2 enter the formula `=I2-H2` Complete column J.

    Your spreadsheet should look like this:

	A	B	C	D	E	F	G	H	I	J	K
1		Mon	Tue	Wed	Thu	Fri	Total sales	Cost price	Sell price	Profit per can	Total profit
2	Cola	10	10	10	10	10	50	£0.15	£0.65	£0.50	
3	Diet Cola	10	10	10	10	10	50	£0.15	£0.65	£0.50	
4	Sunkist	10	10	10	10	10	50	£0.15	£0.65	£0.50	
5	Lilt	10	10	10	10	10	50	£0.15	£0.65	£0.50	
6	Cherry Cola	10	10	10	10	10	50	£0.15	£0.65	£0.50	
7	Total cans sold									Weekly profit	

6. The total profit is calculated by multiplying the total sales by the profit per can. In cell K2 enter the correct formula. Complete column K.

7. Complete the model by entering the correct formulas in cells G7 (total cans sold) and K7 (weekly profit).

8. Check that the figures in your spreadsheet are correct.

■ Entering real data

The school buys in from a wholesaler in Burton at the cost prices shown below.

It decides to sell at 50p per can.

The weekly sales for a week in July are as shown below.

9.   Enter the data into your model

	A	B	C	D	E	F	G	H	I	J	K
1		Mon	Tue	Wed	Thu	Fri	Total sales	Cost price	Sell price	Profit per can	Total profit
2	Cola	23	12	19	24	19	97	£0.17	£0.50	£0.33	
3	Diet Cola	12	16	16	18	19	81	£0.16	£0.50	£0.34	
4	Sunkist	21	17	18	11	18	85	£0.18	£0.50	£0.32	
5	Lilt	17	19	19	13	24	92	£0.18	£0.50	£0.32	
6	Cherry Cola	16	21	20	16	13	86	£0.15	£0.50	£0.35	
7	Total cans sold									Weekly profit	

10. Complete the spreadsheet and save it as **Vending.xls**

11. The school decides to increase all prices by 10p. What would the expected weekly profit be now?

12. The school finds a wholesaler who will supply all cans at 1p cheaper than currently paid. What increase would this make to the total weekly profit?

13. The school wants to operate on a profit of about £175 per week. Use your model to recommend a set of selling prices that will achieve this profit margin. (Prices for different drinks do not have to be the same.)

■ The school play

The school drama society wants to use a spreadsheet to store details of seat bookings and income from the sale of tickets and programmes.

The school hall has seats for 144 people. The seats are arranged in four blocks of six rows with six seats in each row.

The layout is shown below.

	A	B	C	D	E	F	G	H	I	J	K	L	M	N	O	P
1																
2							The Stage									
3																
4																
5																
6																
7																
8																
9																
10																
11																
12																
13																
14																
15																
16																
17																
18																

The cells of the spreadsheet are used for the rows and columns of the seats. Each cell will represent one seat.

When a seat is booked a number 1 is entered in the cell. Seats that are vacant are left blank.

The seats in the front two blocks are priced at £5.00 and the seats in the rear blocks at £3.50.

We will start by setting up the spreadsheet as shown.

1. Highlight columns B to O, and click on **Format, Column, Width** and set the column width to 5.

2. Enter the title into cell B2. Highlight cells B2 to O2 and click on the **Merge and Center** icon to merge the cells for the stage (see page 178).

3. Change the title to a suitable font size.

4. Highlight each of the four blocks of seats in turn and click on **Format, Cells** and click on the **Borders** tab. Click on **Outline** and **Inside** to format the borders.

5. Similarly for each block click on **Format, Cells** and click on the

Patterns tab. Select a suitable fill colour.

6. Design a spreadsheet model to store the number of seats sold in each row, the total number of seats sold and the total income from the sale of seats.

7. Test your model so that as a seat is sold, the total number of seats sold increases by 1 and the income increases accordingly.

8. Extend your spreadsheet to store details of income from programmes sold. Programmes sell at £1.00. Assume that you sell one programme for every two people in the audience.

Save your file as **Play.xls**.

■ Further development

Use **Format, Conditional Formatting** so that the seat changes colour on the screen when it is sold. Sold seats could be red, unsold green.

Workbooks and multiple worksheets

In this chapter you will cover the following features of Excel:

- multiple worksheets;
- copying data between worksheets;
- linking worksheets;
- conditional formatting;
- viewing multiple worksheets;
- custom views;
- grouping worksheets;

■ Introduction

When you start Excel a blank workbook opens with the default title
Book 1.

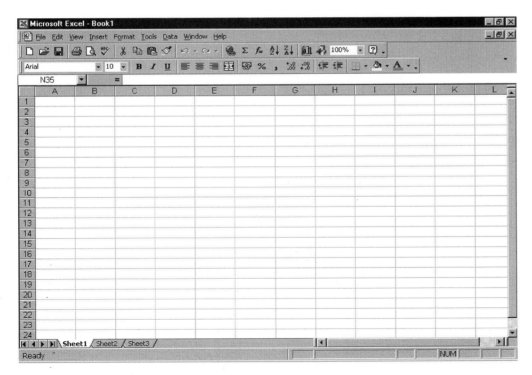

A worksheet is a 'page' in Excel.

A workbook is an Excel file and is like a folder for several worksheets.

It is possible to link these worksheets together to store, share and exchange information.

A typical use might be departmental, financial and numeric data combined to form an overall summary.

Basic worksheet operations

When you open a workbook Sheet1 is the active sheet. You can move between sheets by clicking on the **Sheet tab**.

By default an Excel workbook has three worksheets: Sheet1, Sheet2 and Sheet3. This can easily be changed by clicking on **Tools**, **Options**, clicking on the **General** tab and increasing the number of **Sheets in new workbook** option.

Right clicking on a sheet tab brings up a menu from which it is easy to rename, delete, add and insert sheets.

As ever there are many alternative ways of achieving the same operation.

To change the name of a sheet, double click the sheet tab and type in the new name.

You can insert a new sheet by pressing SHIFT + F11.

You can change the order of the sheets by simply dragging the sheet tab to its new position.

A WORKED EXAMPLE: Annual accounts

The Technology faculty in a large comprehensive school is divided into three departments, ICT, Food and Design Technology.

An annual budget is given to Head of Faculty who delegates a sum of money to each subject head.

Each subject head allocates a sum of money to the budget headings Equipment, Software, Text Books, Stationery, Reprographics, and Repairs.

You are going to set up a workbook to store details of the departmental accounts.

We will use a new worksheet for each department.

Setting up the spreadsheet

	A	B	C	D	E	F	G	H	I	J
1										
2					ICT Dept Accounts 2000/2001					
3			Order	Equipment	Software	Text Books	Stationery	Reprographics	Repairs	Total
4			Number							
5										
6										
7										
8										
9										
10										
11										
12										
13										
14										
15										
16			Total							
17										
18			Budget							
19										
20			Difference							
21										
22										
23										
24										

ICT / Food / Design / Faculty Summary /

1. Enter the row and column headings as shown above.
2. In cell E2 enter the heading ICT Dept Accounts 2000/2001
3. Highlight cells E2 to G2 and click the **Merge and Center** icon.
4. Right click on the **Sheet1** tab and rename it **ICT**. Rename the other two tabs **Food** and **Design**.
5. Click on **Insert, Worksheet** and rename the new worksheet **Faculty Summary**
6. Format the layout as you think suitable.

Save your file as **Accounts.xls**.

Entering the order numbers

1. In cell C5 enter **7500**.
2. Highlight cells C5 to C14 and click on **Edit, Fill** and click on **Series**.
3. Click on **Columns,** choose a step value of 1 and click **OK**.

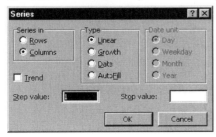

Setting up the formulas

1. In cell J5 enter the formula `=SUM(D5:I5)`

2. Copy and Paste this formula into all the cells from J6 to J14.

3. In D16 enter the formula `=SUM(D5:D14)`

4. Copy and paste the formula into all the cells from E16 to I16.

5. In cells D18 to I18 enter a budget of 0.

6. In cell D20 enter the formula `=D18-D16`

7. Copy and Paste the formula into cells E20 to I20.

8. In cell J16 enter the formula `=SUM(D16:I16)`

9. Copy and Paste this formula into J18 and J20.

10. Highlight cells D5 to J20 and format to currency.

11. Save your file. It should appear as below.

	A	B	C	D	E	F	G	H	I	J
1										
2					ICT Dept Accounts 2000/2001					
3			Order	Equipment	Software	Text Books	Stationery	Reprographics	Repairs	Total
4			Number							
5			7500							£0.00
6			7501							£0.00
7			7502							£0.00
8			7503							£0.00
9			7504							£0.00
10			7505							£0.00
11			7506							£0.00
12			7507							£0.00
13			7508							£0.00
14			7509							£0.00
15										
16			Total	£0.00	£0.00	£0.00	£0.00	£0.00	£0.00	£0.00
17										
18			Budget	£0.00	£0.00	£0.00	£0.00	£0.00	£0.00	£0.00
19										
20			Difference	£0.00	£0.00	£0.00	£0.00	£0.00	£0.00	£0.00

Copy and pasting to other worksheets

1. Highlight the cells **C2** to **J20** and click on the **Copy** icon

2. Move to the sheet named **Food**.

3. Click on cell C2 and click on paste.

4. Edit the heading to read **Food Dept Accounts 2000/2001**.

5. Clear the order numbers by highlighting cells C5 to C14 and clicking on **Edit, Clear, All**.

6. Set the order numbers to be 7600, 7601, 7602,... as shown in the diagrams below.

7. Repeat this process to produce the **Design** accounts and set the order numbers to be 7700, 7701, 7702,...

8. Save your file.

Entering the data

The following screen shots show the budgets and some order details for each department.

1. Enter the orders and budgets into each worksheet as shown. You will need to make column J wider.

ICT accounts

		ICT Dept Accounts 2000/2001				
Order Number	Equipment	Software	Text Books	Stationery	Reprographics	Repairs
7500	£ 100.00					
7501	£ 450.00					
7502		£ 200.00				
7503		£ 100.00				
7504			£ 500.00			
7505				£ 500.00		
7506					£ 600.00	
7507						
7508						
7509						
Total	£ 550.00	£ 300.00	£ 500.00	£ 500.00	£ 600.00	£ -
Budget	£ 500.00	£ 500.00	£ 1,000.00	£ 1,500.00	£ 1,000.00	£ -
Difference	-£ 50.00	£ 200.00	£ 500.00	£ 1,000.00	£ 400.00	£ -

Food accounts

Order Number	Equipment	Software	Text Books	Stationery	Reprographics	Repairs
		Food Dept Accounts 2000/2001				
7600	£ 200.00					
7601		£ 200.00				
7602			£ 450.00			
7603				£ 400.00		
7604					£ 300.00	
7605						£ 250.00
7606						
7607						
7608						
7609						
Total	£ 200.00	£ 200.00	£ 450.00	£ 400.00	£ 300.00	£ 250.00
Budget	£ 1,000.00	£ 200.00	£ 500.00	£ 500.00	£ 700.00	£ 500.00

Design accounts

Order Number	Equipment	Software	Text Books	Stationery	Reprographics	Repairs
		Design Dept Accounts 2000/2001				
7700	£ 1,500.00					
7701		£ 200.00				
7702			£ 800.00			
7703				£ 300.00		
7704					£ 400.00	
7705						£ 700.00
7706						
7707						
7708						
7709						
Total	£ 1,500.00	£ 200.00	£ 800.00	£ 300.00	£ 400.00	£ 700.00
Budget	£ 2,000.00	£ 300.00	£ 1,200.00	£ 400.00	£ 600.00	£ 1,000.00

Save your file.

Linking the sheets

We are going to use the sheet named **Faculty Summary** to display the total expenditure of different departments

Switch to the Faculty Summary sheet and set out the row and column headings as overleaf.

	A	B	C	D	E	F	G	H	I	J
1										
2					Faculty of Technology Accounts 2000/2001					
3			Equipment	Software	Text Books	Stationery	Reprographics	Repairs	Total	Budget
4										
5		ICT								
6		Food								
7		Design								
8										
9		Total								

In cell C5 we wish to set up an external reference to cell D16 on the ICT sheet.

1. Click on C5 and enter **=**

2. Switch to the ICT sheet and click on D16. The formula should read `=ICT!D16` Press ENTER.

3. C6 will contain `=Food!D16`

4. C7 will contain `=Design!D16`

5. In C9 we need to total the equipment expenditure for each department. Add the contents of C5, C6 and C7 in cell C9. You will probably use the formula `=SUM(C5:C7)` but you could use `=ICT!D16+Food!D16+Design!D16`

Any cell can be referenced in this way. Each external reference must follow the format full sheet name plus the cell reference separated by an exclamation mark.

6. Complete the spreadsheet as shown. Using Copy and Paste will save you time.

Save your file.

	A	B	C	D	E	F	G	H	I	J
1										
2					Faculty of Technology Accounts 2000/2001					
3			Equipment	Software	Text Books	Stationery	Reprographics	Repairs	Total	Budget
4										
5		ICT	£ 550.00	£ 300.00	£ 500.00	£ 500.00	£ 600.00	£0.00	£2,450.00	£ 4,500.00
6		Food	£ 200.00	£ 200.00	£ 450.00	£ 400.00	£ 300.00	£ 250.00	£1,800.00	£ 3,400.00
7		Design	£ 1,500.00	£ 200.00	£ 800.00	£ 300.00	£ 400.00	£ 700.00	£3,900.00	£ 5,500.00
8										
9		Total	£ 2,250.00	£ 700.00	£ 1,750.00	£1,200.00	£ 1,300.00	£ 950.00	£8,150.00	£ 13,400.00

Conditional formatting

You can use conditional formatting to highlight cells that meet certain criteria.

When there is an overspend on budget we might wish to highlight that cell or range of cells in a different colour or font.

1. Turn to the ICT worksheet and click on cell D20.

2. Click on **Format, Conditional Formatting**.

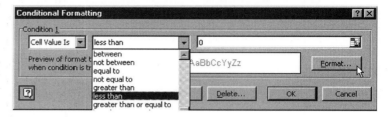

3. Choose **less than** from the drop down list and set the value to 0.

4. Click on **Format** and set the font colour to red.

5. There is an overspend and so the cell is highlighted. Complete by applying formatting across the rest of the cells.

Note: Sometimes it is hard to tell where you have applied conditional formatting.

Click on **Edit, GoTo, Special** and check **Conditional formats**. Click on **OK**.

The cells with conditional formatting will be highlighted.

Viewing multiple sheets

To view more than one sheet from the same workbook at a time, open a new window for each sheet you wish to view.

From the menu click on **Window, New Window**. Nothing appears to happen yet! Change to a different worksheet by clicking on the sheet tab.

We have four worksheets to view so repeat the **Window, New Window** operation two more times, each time selecting a different worksheet.

Click on **Window, Arrange** to display the dialog box below.

Choose the way you wish to view your worksheets, we have chosen tiled

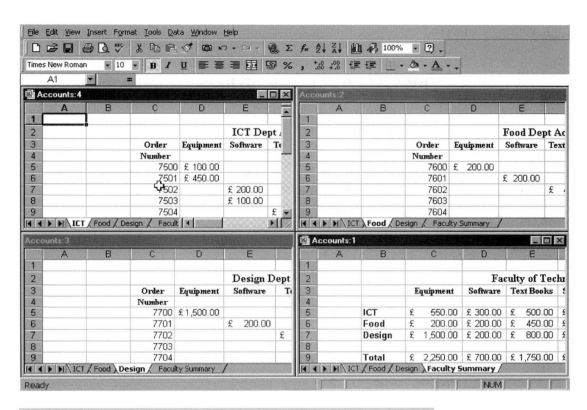

Using custom views

You may wish to return regularly and quickly to the tiled view
previously used.

Click on **View, Custom Views**

Click on **Add** and call the view **Overview**

Whenever you wish to return to the custom view, from the menu click
on **View, Custom Views** and choose **Overview.**

Grouping sheets

If a number of sheets are going to contain the same headings, data and format, it might be quicker to work with grouped sheets.

Every operation carried out on the active sheet is copied across to the sheets in the selected group.

Select adjacent sheets by clicking on the tab of the leftmost sheet, hold down shift and click on the tab of the rightmost sheet.

To include non-adjacent sheets, hold down CTRL while clicking the sheet tab of the sheets you wish to include.

You can turn off sheet grouping by right clicking the sheet tab of the sheet you wish to become active and select ungroup sheet from the short cut menu.

Using AutoFormat on grouped sheets

1. Select all the sheets as a group.

2. On the ICT sheet highlight cells C2 to J20.

3. Click on **Format, AutoFormat** and click on style **Classic 2**.

4. On the ICT worksheet in cell J22 enter the heading **Date**.

5. On the ICT worksheet in cell J23 enter the function `=TODAY()`

6. Adjust the column widths as necessary.

Save your file as **Accountsstyle.xls**.

	B	C	D	E	F	G	H	I	J
1									
2					ICT Dept Accounts 2000/2001				
3		Order	Equipment	Software	Text Books	Stationery	Reprographics	Repairs	**Total**
4		Number							
5		7500	£ 100.00						£ 100.00
6		7501	£ 450.00						£ 450.00
7		7502		£ 200.00					£ 200.00
8		7503		£ 100.00					£ 100.00
9		7504			£ 500.00				£ 500.00
10		7505				£ 500.00			£ 500.00
11		7506					£ 600.00		£ 600.00
12		7507							£ -
13		7508							£ -
14		7509							£ -
15									
16		Total	£ 550.00	£ 300.00	£ 500.00	£ 500.00	£ 600.00	£ -	£2,450.00
17									
18		Budget	£ 500.00	£ 500.00	£ 1,000.00	£ 1,500.00	£ 1,000.00	£ -	£4,500.00
19									
20		*Difference*	-£ 50.00	£ 200.00	£ 500.00	£ 1,000.00	£ 400.00	£ -	£2,050.00
21									
22									29/10/00
23									

Printing in Excel

In this chapter you will cover the following features

- printing a worksheet;
- printing with multiple worksheets;
- printing a header and footer;
- printing the gridlines and row and column headings;
- draft quality and black and white printing;
- reusing the row and column headings on subsequent pages;
- adjusting the size of your page to fit;
- landscape and portrait printing;
- scaling the page;
- adjusting the print margins;
- setting the print area;
- inserting a page break;

■ 1. Printing a worksheet

1. Click on **File**, **Print** to call up the standard printing dialog box.

2. Choose your number of copies by incrementing the **Number of copies** control.

3. Choose your page range by either selecting **All** the pages or choosing a **Print range** by adjusting the **From To** controls.

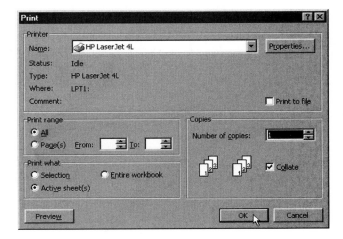

■ 2. Printing with multiple worksheets

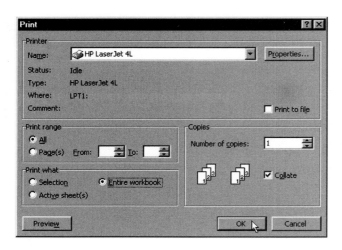

1. Click on **File, Print** to call up the standard printing dialog box.

2. Check **Entire workbook** to print out every sheet in the workbook which contains data, (blank sheets are not included); or

3. Check **Active sheet(s)** to print only selected sheets. Hold down CTRL and click on the sheet tabs you wish to print.

Hint:

■ Using **File, Print Preview** before printing can save a lot of wasted paper.

■ 3. Printing a header and footer

Use headers and footers to print information, such as the title or the page number.

If a worksheet has several pages of print-out, the header and footer will appear on all of them. You can customise the header and footer to include information you want printed on each page.

1. Click on **File, Page Setup** to call up the standard **Page Setup** dialog box.

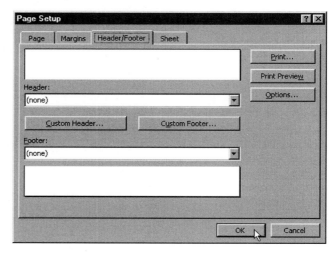

2. Click on the **Header/Footer** tab and select **Custom Header**.

The header is in three sections, Left, Centre and Right. You can use whichever you think is suitable.

✈ Add text by typing in any of the sections.

✈ To add a page number, click on the second (#) icon. It appears on screen as **&[Page]**.

✈ To add the date, click on the fourth (calendar) icon. It appears on screen as **&[Date]**.

✈ To add the time, click on the fifth (clock) icon. It appears on screen as **&[Time]**.

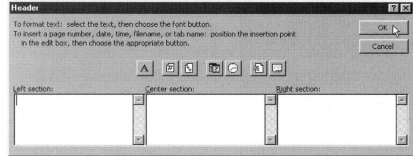

> **Note**
> ■ You can use the built-in drop down list to choose a header
> ■ It is common to number pages in the footer and to put a title and your name in the header.
> ■ You cannot insert graphics or cell references into a header or footer.
> ■ Use **Custom Footer...** to set up the footer in the same way.

■ 4. Printing the Gridlines and Row and Column Headings

1. Click on **File, Page Setup** to call up the standard **Page Setup** dialog box.

2. Click on the **Sheet** tab.

3. Check the **Gridlines** and the **Row and Column headings** box.

If you want greater control over the gridlines then you can easily place a border around your cells.

Click **Format, Cells** and click the **Border** tab to give a range of types, styles and colours.

To remove, simply click **No Border**.

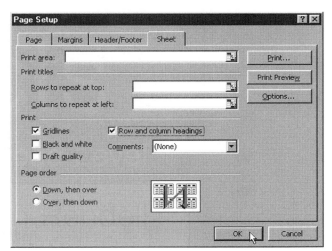

Other options available from the Page Setup, Sheet dialog box

Check **Draft Quality** to speed up the printing of graphics.
Worksheets with lots of graphic images can slow printing down;
if you are prepared to lose a little quality you can gain speed.

Check **Black and White**. If you have done a lot of graph/chart work
with colours and have a black and white printer it is better to print as
a black and white image. Excel substitutes the colours with a range of
grey tones and gives you a crisper image.

Reusing the row and column headings on subsequent pages

If your spreadsheet carries on to another page then you can lock the
headings to appear on the next page.

With the **Sheet** tab clicked on the **Page Setup** dialog box

1.   Click in the Rows to repeat at top box

2.   Click on the row number you wish to be the header and click **OK**

■ 5. Adjusting the size of your page
to fit

Click on **File, Page Setup** and then click on the **Page** tab.

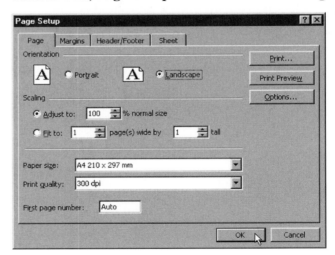

☐ Landscape and portrait printing

Printing in landscape mode is often more suitable as it reflects the
shape of the screen. Set the Orientation to either portrait or landscape.

Scaling the page

Click the **Adjust to** option to reduce your worksheet to a specific percentage. For example if you set it at 85% then every item on the worksheet would be reduced to 85% of its original size

Alternatively if you set the **Fit to** option 1 wide by 1 tall Excel will reduce the worksheet by whatever percentage is needed to fit everything to the page.

■ 6. Adjusting the print margins

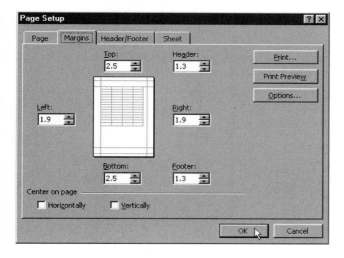

1. Click on **File, Page Setup** to call up the standard **Page Setup** dialog box.

2. Click on the margin controls to reduce the white space around the edge of your spreadsheet.

3. Check the horizontal and vertical control boxes to position as required.

■ 7. Setting the print area

If you don't want to print the whole worksheet area but just a part of it then

1.   Highlight the area to be printed.

2.   Click **File, Print Area, Set Print Area**.

A dashed line should appear around your print area. To clear click **File, Print Area, Clear Print Area**.

■ 8. Inserting a page break

Page breaks can be viewed by clicking **Tools, Options** and checking **Page Breaks**. To set your own:

1.   Place the cursor in Column A below the row where you wish to insert the page break.

2.   Click **Insert, Page Break**.

A horizontal dashed line will appear across the worksheet.

To remove the page break place the cursor in the row below the page break and click **Insert, Remove Page Break**.

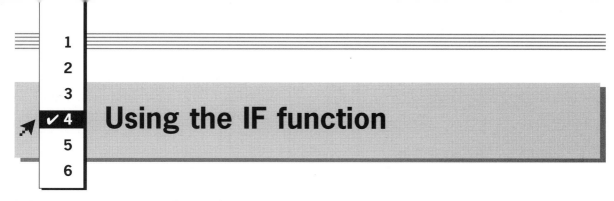

Using the IF function

In this chapter you will cover the following features of Excel:

the **IF** function;

nested **IFs**.

■ Introduction

The **IF** function tests the value in a cell and does one thing if the test is true and another if the test is false.

The function has three arguments: the test, the action to carry out if true and the action to carry out if false.

The format is **IF(logical test, action if true, action if false)**.

Try this:

1. Enter 7 in cell A1.

2. Select Cell B4 and enter the following
   `=IF(A1=0,"TRUE", "FALSE")`

Excel looks at A1 and checks its value. A1 is not zero so it ignores the first action and returns FALSE in B4.

B4	▼	= =IF(A1=0,"TRUE","FALSE")		
A	B	C	D	E
1	7			
2				
3				
4	FALSE			
5				

3. Enter 0 in A1 and Excel will return the first action TRUE in B4.

Further examples of using IF

Cell D5 contains a formula to calculate departmental expenditure:

`=IF(D5>= 1000, "over budget ", "")`

The function will return over budget if D5 is greater than or equal to 1000 and a blank if not.

Cell C10 is named MARK and stores the exam mark for a student:

`=IF(MARK<50,"fail","pass")`

The function will return fail if MARK is less than 50 and pass if it is greater than or equal to 50.

The format of the **IF** function can be quite complex involving functions and formulas:

=IF(A10=1000, SUM(C5:C10), "")

=IF(B2>100,B2,B3-B2)

=IF(B2=0,B1/B2,B1+B2)

WORKED EXAMPLE 1:   Football results

Set up the spreadsheet as below with the results as shown.

	A	B	C	D	E	F
1						
2		Home	For	Away	Against	Result
3						
4		Arsenal	3	Barcelona	2	
5		Lazio	2	AC Milan	1	
6		Celtic	0	Bruges	1	
7						

We are going to use the **IF** function to display whether the result was a home win, an away win or a draw. We will use the **Function Wizard** although, if you prefer, formulas can be entered manually

We need to compare cells C4 and E4. If C4 is greater than E4 then clearly the result is a home win. The formula needed is

=IF(C4>E4,"Home","Away")

1. Position the cursor in cell F4.

2. From the **Insert** menu, select **Function**.

3. Select **IF** from the functions displayed.

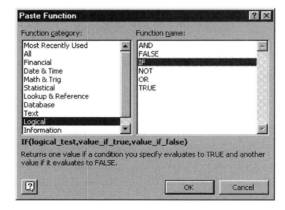

4. Enter the details as shown. The speech marks are inserted automatically for text but are not needed for numbers. Click on **OK**.

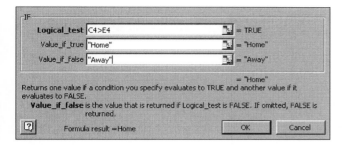

5. Copy and paste the formula to cell F6 to produce the spreadsheet below.

	A	B	C	D	E	F
1						
2		Home	For	Away	Against	Result
3						
4		Arsenal	3	Barcelona	2	Home
5		Lazio	2	AC Milan	1	Home
6		Celtic	0	Bruges	1	Away
7						

Save your file as **Football.xls**.

■ Further development

The **IF** function so far has operated on only two outcomes. Clearly, however, in a football match there can be a draw.

To solve this we use a **nested IF** statement. The logic here is a little more complex.

We compare cells C4 and E4. If C4>E4 then it is a Home win. If it is not, we use another **IF** statement to decide if C4 =E4. If it is, the result is a Draw. If not the remaining action must be an Away win.

The formula needed is =IF(C4>E4,"Home",IF(C4=E4,"Draw","Away"))

Enter the formula in cell F4 and copy and paste into F5 and F6.

Test by changing the score of the Celtic game to 1–1 as shown below.

Save your file.

F4	▼	=	=IF(C4>E4,"Home",IF(C4=E4, "","Away"))		
	A	B	C	D	E	F
1						
2		Home	For	Away	Against	Result
3						
4		Arsenal	3	Barcelona	2	Home
5		Lazio	2	AC Milan	1	Home
6		Celtic	1	Bruges	1	Draw

▶ WORKED EXAMPLE 2:   A mobile phone bill

A mobile phone company have two tariffs for their contract customers called tariff A and B. The rates are shown below.

Tariff	Peak rate	Off-peak rate	Line rental
A	30p	5p	£15.00
B	10p	2p	£20.00

A customer also pays line rental according to the tariff used.

Set up the spreadsheet as shown below.

	A	B	C	D
1				
2	**Mobile Phone Account**			
3				
4		Minutes	Price per minute	Cost
5	Call charges (peak)	147		
6	Call charges (off peak)	94		
7	Line rental			
8	Total			
9	VAT			
10	Total with VAT			
11				
12	Tariff			
13	A			

In cells C5 andC6 we need an IF statement to enter the correct price dependent on the tariff used in A13.

1. In C5 enter =IF(A13="A",0.30,0.10)

2. In C6 enter =IF(A13="A",0.05,0.02)

In D7 we need an IF statement to enter the line rental charge dependent on the tariff used in A13.

3. In D7 enter =IF(A13= "A",15.00,20.00)

Set up the formulas to complete the spreadsheet as shown below; VAT is charged at 17.5%.

Save your file as **Mobile.xls**.

	A	B	C	D
1				
2	**Mobile Phone Account**			
3				
4		Minutes	Price per minute	Cost
5	Call Charges (peak)	147	£0.30	£44.10
6	Call Charges (off peak)	94	£0.05	£4.70
7	Line rental			£15.00
8	Total			£63.80
9	VAT			£11.17
10	Total with VAT			£74.97
11				
12	Tariff			
13	A			

■ Further development

LPX Mobile have announced a new tariff, tariff C.

Tariff	Peak rate	Off-peak rate	Line rental
C	9p	free	£30

This means there are now three tariffs and we need to use a nested IF statement. We must alter the formula in C5 that is currently `=IF(A13="A", 0.30,0.10)` to the following

`=IF(A13="C",0.09,IF(A13="A",0.30,0.10))`

The logic is as follows. Excel looks at A13, if it is Tariff C then it returns 9p, if it is not it tests to see if it is Tariff A. If it is, it returns 30p else it must be Tariff B in which case 10p is returned.

Complete the nested IFs for cells C6 and D7. The spreadsheet should appear as on the right.

Save your file.

	A	B	C	D
1				
2	**Mobile Phone Account**			
3				
4		Minutes	Price per minute	Cost
5	Call charges (peak)	147	£0.09	£13.23
6	Call charges (off peak)	94	£0.00	£ -
7	Line rental			£30.00
8	Total			£43.23
9	VAT			£7.57
10	Total with VAT			£50.80
11				
12	Tariff			
13	C			

▶ IF function exercise

1. The grade boundaries for coursework submissions are given in the table below

Grade Boundary	Grade
65-90	Merit
42-64	Pass
0-41	Fail

The spreadsheet below shows a section of a teacher's markbook. Use nested IFs to calculate the grades from the marks shown.

	A	B	C
1	**Coursework marks**		
2			
3			
4		Module 3	Grade
5	Daniel Shone	70	
6	Tom Millington	66	
7	Bryan Land	52	
8	Kevin Fisher	56	
9	Peter Adams	44	
10	David Taylor	40	
11	Susan Welch	56	

Statistical functions

In this chapter you will learn about some of the statistical functions available in Excel.

■ Introduction

The table below shows some of the more commonly used functions

MAX	Finds the number with the highest value in a given range
MIN	Finds the number with the lowest value in a given range
AVERAGE	Finds the average of numbers in a given range
SUMIF	Adds the cells that meet a certain criteria
COUNT	Finds the number of cells containing numbers in a given range
COUNTA	Finds the number of cells containing text or numbers in a given range
COUNTIF	Counts the number of cells in a range that meet a certain criteria
COUNTBLANK	Counts the empty cells in a given range

▶ A WORKED EXAMPLE: A Teacher's Markbook

	A	B	C	D	E
1	Unit test marks %				
2	GCE Advanced ICT Group 12A				
3					
4		Unit 1	Grade	Analysis	
5	Daniel Shone	76	A		
6	Phillip Webster	80	A	Number of students	=COUNTA(A5:A18)
7	Tom Millington	68	A	Number of entries	=COUNT(B5:B18)
8	Amy Jackson	64	A	Non entries	=COUNTBLANK(B5:B18)
9	Bryan Land	52	C	Highest mark	=MAX(B5:B18)
10	Gemma Pegg	50	C	Lowest mark	=MIN(B5:B18)
11	Kevin Fisher	54	B	Average mark	=AVERAGE(B5:B18)
12	Edward Short	46	C	Ungraded	=COUNTIF(C5:C18,"U")
13	Peter Adams	44	C		
14	David Taylor	40	C		
15	Robert White	42	D		
16	Susan Welch	56	C		
17	David Lloyd	32	U		
18	Adam Drabble	28	U		

This example will explain how to use the **Average** function

1. Set up the markbook shown below by entering the data in columns A to D only.

2. Position the cursor in E11.

3. Click **Insert, Function, Statistical**.

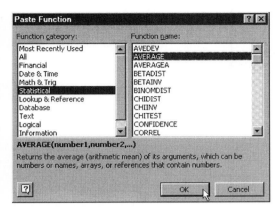

4. Scrolling through you will see a range of statistical functions.
    Click **Average**.

5. This displays the **Function box**.
    Enter B5:B18 or simply highlight the cells.

NB You can of course just enter the function without using the
Function Wizard.

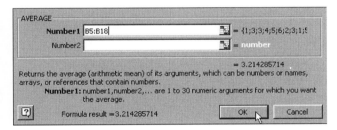

Complete the statistical analysis as shown by whichever method you
prefer. The results are shown below. Save your file as **Markbook.xls**.

	A	B	C	D	E
1	Unit test marks %				
2	GCE Advanced ICT Group 12A				
3					
4		Unit 1	Grade	Analysis	
5	Daniel Shone	76	A		
6	Phillip Webster	80	A	Number of students	14
7	Tom Millington	68	A	Number of entries	14
8	Amy Jackson	64	A	Non entries	0
9	Bryan Land	52	C	Highest mark	80
10	Gemma Pegg	50	C	Lowest mark	28
11	Kevin Fisher	54	B	Average mark	52.29
12	Edward Short	46	C	Ungraded	2
13	Peter Adams	44	C		
14	David Taylor	40	C		
15	Robert White	42	D		
16	Susan Welch	56	C		
17	David Lloyd	32	U		
18	Adam Drabble	28	U		

Statistical function exercise

1. A teacher keeps a register in her markbook. Use the statistical functions available to produce an attendance report for the teacher.

	A	B	C	D	E	F	G	H	I	J	K	L	M	N	O	P	Q	R	S	T
1	Attendance Register																			
2	GCE Advanced ICT Group12A																			
3		5-Sep	6-Sep	7-Sep	8-Sep	9-Sep	12-Sep	13-Sep	14-Sep	15-Sep	16-Sep	19-Sep	20-Sep	21-Sep	22-Sep	23-Sep	26-Sep	27-Sep	28-Sep	29-Sep
4	Daniel Shone	1	0	1	1	1	1	1	1	1	1	1	1	1	1	1	1	1	0	1
5	Phillip Webster	1	1	1	1	1	0	1	1	0	1	1	1	0	1	1	0	1	1	0
6	Tom Millington	1	1	0	1	1	1	1	1	1	1	1	1	1	1	1	1	1	1	0
7	Amy Jackson	1	1	1	1	1	1	1	1	1	1	1	1	1	1	1	1	1	1	1
8	Bryan Land	1	1	1	1	1	1	1	1	1	1	1	1	1	1	1	1	1	1	1
9	Gemma Pegg	1	1	1	0	1	0	1	1	1	1	0	1	0	1	1	1	1	1	1
10	Kevin Fisher	0	1	1	1	1	1	1	1	1	1	1	1	1	1	1	1	0	1	0
11	Edward Short	1	1	1	1	1	1	1	1	1	1	1	1	1	1	1	1	1	1	1
12	Peter Adams	1	1	1	1	1	1	1	1	1	1	1	1	1	1	1	1	1	1	0
13	David Taylor	1	1	1	1	1	1	1	1	1	1	1	1	1	1	1	1	1	1	1
14	Robert White	1	1	1	1	1	1	1	0	1	0	1	1	1	0	1	1	1	1	1
15	Susan Welch	1	1	1	1	1	1	1	1	1	1	1	1	1	1	1	1	1	1	1

2. The Geography Department run a school weather station and take daily readings as shown below. The results are keyed into a spreadsheet. Use the statistical functions available to produce a weekly weather report for the area.

Weather readings for week ending 21/10/00

	Mon	Tue	Wed	Thur	Fri	Sat	Sun
Temperature (C$^{\circ}$)	12	13	15	12	12	12	11
Rainfall (mm)	0	0	4	3	2	0	0
Pressure (Mb)	996	1000	1000	888	992	946	1004
Sunshine (hrs)	1	2	2	1	1	2	2

Hints for Question 1:
- Percentage attendance.
- Best/worst attendance figures.
- Number of absences.
- Best/worst absence records.
- Absence patterns.
- Projected figures.
- Figures given individually or for the group.

Data validation and cell protection

■ Data validation

In this section you will learn how to use **data validation** to ensure that only reasonable and sensible data is entered into a cell.

Introduction

To view the **Data Validation** option click **Data, Validation** and ensure the **Settings** tab is clicked.

Click on the **Allow** drop down to view the options.

⤢ Numbers can be restricted to whole numbers or decimals. Click on the **Data** drop down to view the criteria and limit options.

⤢ Dates and times can be controlled in the same way.

⤢ Text entry can be restricted to a number of characters.

⤢ Valid entries can also be selected from a list.

⤢ You can custom build controls based on functions and formulae.

Data Validation ? ✕

| Settings | Input Message | Error Alert |

Validation criteria

Allow:

Any value ▾   ☑ Ignore blank

Any value
Whole number
Decimal
List
Date
Time
Text length
Custom

☐ Apply these changes to all other cells with the same settings

Clear All   OK   Cancel

▷ A WORKED EXAMPLE: Student details

Set up the spreadsheet as below to enter student details.

	A	B	C	D
1				
2		Student Details		
3				
4		Surname		
5		Forename		
6		Sex		
7		Year		
8		Form		
9		DOB		
10				
11				

▶

Validating the surname

1. Select C4 and click **Data, Validation**.

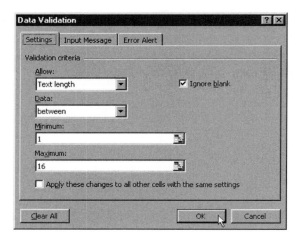

2. Click **Text length** in the **Allow** drop down.

3. Select **between** from the **Data** drop down.

4. Set **Maximum** and **Minimum** values to 16 and 1 character.

5. Click the **Input Message** tab and enter the details as below.

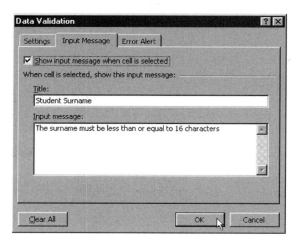

6. Click the **Error Alert** tab and enter the details as below.

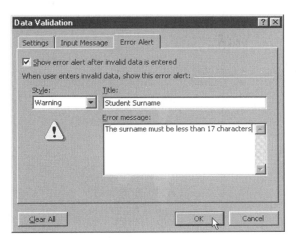

7. Test the validation check by entering a name over 16 characters in C4.

Validating the form

1. Select C8 and click **Data, Validation**.

2. Click **List** in the **Allow** drop down.

3. Enter the names of the forms separated by commas in the **Source** box as shown right.

4. Set up a suitable **Input Message** and **Error Alert**; click **OK**.

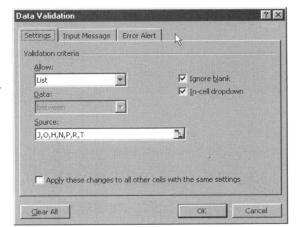

You will notice a drop down appears from which you can enter the form.

NB The list option is very powerful. If the list is long or likely to change then enter the list range on another part of the sheet and name the range.

When setting up the validation check enter the name in the **Source** box. You will cover cell naming in greater detail later.

	A	B	C	D
1				
2		**Student Details**		
3				
4		Surname	Bowles	
5		Forename	Stanley	
6		Sex	M	
7		Year		11
8		Form	P	
9		DOB		12/12/85
10				
11				

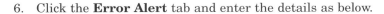

Exercise 6.1

Validation exercise

1. Complete suitable validation checks for all data in the above example. Is it possible to copy and paste validation controls ?

2. In Unit 1 we set up the worksheet called **Mileage.xls**.

Set up a suitable validation check for the miles per gallon in cell A1. The mpg should lie between 50 and 15 inclusive.

NB Whenever we add validation, we must test that it works. You will need to test it with data that is valid and with data that is invalid.

In this example you would need to check that:

(a) Numbers bigger than 50 are rejected – test it with 51;

(b) Numbers smaller than 15 are rejected – test it with 14;

(c) 15 and 50 are accepted.

	A	B	C
1	37	mpg	
2			
3	miles	gallons	litres
4	1000	27.03	122.70
5	2000	54.05	245.41
6	3000	81.08	368.11
7	4000	108.11	490.81
8	5000	135.14	613.51
9	6000	162.16	736.22
10	7000	189.19	858.92
11	8000	216.22	981.62
12	9000	243.24	1104.32
13	10000	270.27	1227.03
14	11000	297.30	1349.73
15	12000	324.32	1472.43

■ Cell protection

In this section we will see how **cell protection** can prevent cells being changed, either accidentally or mischievously, by the user.

You can protect selected cells or a whole worksheet. It is possible to set up cell protection so that it can only be changed if you know a password.

Protecting a whole worksheet

1. Load Excel and click on **Tools, Protection, Protect Sheet.** The box below appears.

Protect Sheet

Protect worksheet for
- ☑ Contents
- ☑ Objects
- ☑ Scenarios

Password (optional):

[OK] [Cancel]

2. Enter a password here if required, but it is probably not a good idea – you may forget it. You will be asked to re-enter it as verification.

3. If you now try to enter data into any cell, you will not be able to do so and will get an error message.

To turn off protection, click on **Tools Protection, Unprotect Sheet...**
If you have used a password, you will be prompted to type it in now.

▶ A WORKED EXAMPLE: Protecting part of a worksheet

You will need to load the ICT Dept Accounts file used in Unit 2 called
Accounts.xls.

	Order Number	Equipment	Software	Text Books	Stationery	Reprographics	Repairs	Total
			ICT Dept Accounts 2000/2001					
5	7500	£ 100.00						£ 100.00
6	7501	£ 450.00						£ 450.00
7	7502		£ 200.00					£ 200.00
8	7503		£ 100.00					£ 100.00
9	7504			£ 500.00				£ 500.00
10	7505				£ 500.00			£ 500.00
11	7506					£ 600.00		£ 600.00
12	7507							£ -
13	7508							£ -
14	7509							£ -
16	Total	£ 550.00	£ 300.00	£ 500.00	£ 500.00	£ 600.00	£ -	£ 2,450.00
18	Budget	£ 500.00	£ 500.00	£ 1,000.00	£ 1,500.00	£ 1,000.00	£ -	£ 4,500.00
20	Difference	-£ 50.00	£ 200.00	£ 500.00	£ 1,000.00	£ 400.00	£ -	£ 2,050.00

If you only want to protect some cells on a worksheet,
you must first decide which cells you do **NOT** want to
protect. Clearly in this case it is the cells containing
the data. N.B. Ignore passwords in this exercise.

1. Highlight all the cells that you want to allow to
    be changed. Highlight C5 to I14.

2. Click on **Format, Cells**.

3. Click on the **Protection** tab.

4. Remove the tick from the **Locked** box and click
    on OK.

5. Protect the worksheet in the normal way with
    Tools, Protection, **Protect Sheet.**

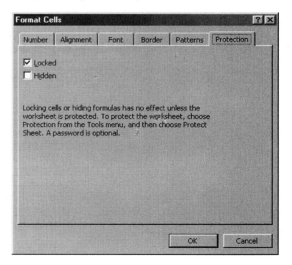

The LOOKUP function and combo boxes

In this chapter, you will learn how to take data from a table and insert it in your spreadsheet using:

➤ naming cells.

➤ LOOKUP functions.

➤ combo boxes.

Naming cells

	A	B	C	D	E
1	No	Max weight (g)	Europe	World Zone 1	World Zone 2
2	1	100	£0.87	£1.15	£1.15
3	2	120	£0.96	£1.32	£1.34
4	3	140	£1.05	£1.49	£1.53
5	4	160	£1.14	£1.66	£1.72
6	5	180	£1.23	£1.83	£1.91
7	6	200	£1.32	£2.00	£2.10

We can give a name to any cell or range of cells. This can make it much easier to find required data.

1. In a new workbook, enter this data showing the cost of sending a small packet abroad.

(The numbers in column A are important as we shall see later.)

2. Highlight the cells from A2 to E7 and click on **Insert, Name, Define**. Enter the name **weight**.

3. On Sheet2 set up this table, defining which countries are in which zone for postage.

	A	B	C
1	No	Country	Zone
2	1	Australia	World Zone 2
3	2	Canada	World Zone 1
4	3	France	Europe
5	4	Germany	Europe
6	5	Israel	World Zone 1
7	6	Italy	Europe
8	7	Japan	World Zone 2
9	8	New Zealand	World Zone 2
10	9	Spain	Europe
11	10	USA	World Zone 1

4. Highlight the cells from A2 to C11 and click on **Insert, Name, Define**. Enter the name **zone**.

5. Save the workbook as **Postage1.xls**.

One reason for naming cells is that if you click on the Name Box drop down arrow, a list of all the named ranges appears as shown below. Click on **weight** to go to the weight table as shown below.

		= Australia	
B2	▼		
weight			C
zone			Zone
2	1	Australia	World Zone 2
3	2	Canada	World Zone 1
4	3	France	Europe
5	4	Germany	Europe
6	5	Israel	World Zone 1
7	6	Italy	Europe
8	7	Japan	World Zone 2
9	8	New Zealand	World Zone 2
10	9	Spain	Europe
11	10	USA	World Zone 1

▶ The LOOKUP function

The lookup function looks up data in a table.

There are three lookup functions, **LOOKUP, VLOOKUP** and **HLOOKUP.** We will concentrate on the most commonly-used function, VLOOKUP (Vertical look-up).

HLOOKUP and LOOKUP are very similar and may be worth investigating further later.

An example of using a LOOKUP, referring to the table on the right would be:

	A	B	C
1	No	Country	Zone
2	1	Australia	World Zone 2
3	2	Canada	World Zone 1
4	3	France	Europe
5	4	Germany	Europe
6	5	Israel	World Zone 1
7	6	Italy	Europe
8	7	Japan	World Zone 2
9	8	New Zealand	World Zone 2
10	9	Spain	Europe
11	10	USA	World Zone 1

`=VLOOKUP(7,A2:C11,2)`

`7` is the value to be looked up.

`A2:C11` is the range where the lookup takes place.

`2` is the column where the value is found.

▶ WORKED EXAMPLE: LOOKUP function

1.   Enter `=VLOOKUP(2,A2:C11,3)` into cell F10.

It looks in the table between cell A2 and cell C11, going to the first column of the table (column A) shown above until it finds the row with `2` in it.

It then finds the data in this row in column `3` of the table.

2.   Check that it returns the value `World Zone 1`.

You can use named ranges of cells in a lookup function. For example, this lookup could be written as

`=VLOOKUP(2,zone,3)`

3. Check that if you enter =VLOOKUP(2,zone,3) into F10 it still returns the value World Zone 1

4. Switch back to Sheet1. Enter =VLOOKUP(4,weight,5) into cell G2. Check that the value is £1.72

> **Note**
>
> ■ The first column of the table must be in **alphabetical or numerical order** for LOOKUP to work.

▶ Combo boxes

A **combo box** (sometimes called a drop down box) is a list of items from which you can choose one piece of data.

To set up a combo box:

1. Load the workbook **Postage1.xls** and switch to a Sheet2.

2. Turn on the Forms toolbar. **View, Toolbars, Forms**

3. Click on the Combo Box icon and drag out a box on the screen near cells E4 and F4.

4. Right click on the box and click on **Format Control**. The dialog box below appears.

5. In the Input Range box enter B2:B11

6. In the Cell Link box type in the cell which will store the data from the Combo Box, E2

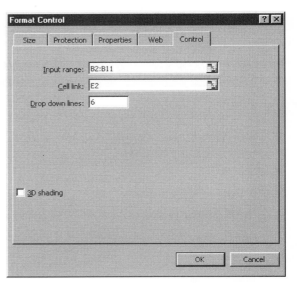

7. Change the **Drop down** lines to 6

8. Click on OK.

9. Save your work.

Hints

■ If you hold the ALT key down, you will align the combo box with the cell gridlines.

■ The smallest height for a combo box is slightly more than the default height for a cell.

If you click on the arrow on your Combo box, you get six lines of different choices like this:

If you choose the fourth item on the list (Germany) cell E2 changes to 4.

	A	B	C	D	E	F
1	No	Country	Zone			
2	1	Australia	World Zone 2		4	
3	2	Canada	World Zone 1			
4	3	France	Europe		Germany ▼	

■ LOOKUP and combo boxes

The lookup function becomes more powerful when combined with a combo box.

> **Remember**
> ■ When you choose an item in a combo box list, the linked cell stores the number of that item, not the item itself.

▶ WORKED EXAMPLE: LOOKUP and combo box

1. Load the file **Postage1.xls** if not already loaded and go to Sheet2.

2. Enter 6 into cell E2 . Enter =VLOOKUP(E2,zone,2) into cell F2.

	A	B	C	D	E	F
1	No	Country	Zone			
2	1	Australia	World Zone 2			6 =VLOOKUP(E2,zone,2)
3	2	Canada	World Zone 1			
4	3	France	Europe		Italy ▼	
5	4	Germany	Europe			
6	5	Israel	World Zone 1			
7	6	Italy	Europe			
8	7	Japan	World Zone 2			
9	8	New Zealand	World Zone 2			
10	9	Spain	Europe			
11	10	USA	World Zone 1			

This looks in **E2** and finds the value **6**. Then it looks in the first column (column A) in the **zone** table shown above until it finds the row with **6** in it. It then finds the data in this row in column **2** of the table. It will return the value Italy

3. Check it returns the value Italy

4. Change the value of E2 to 9 Check that Spain appears in cell F2.

5. Using the combo box click on NewZealand Check that New Zealand appears in F2.

6. Enter =VLOOKUP(E2,zone,3) into cell G2

7. Save your file.

8. Test that as you select a country using the combo box, the zone for that country appears in G2.

Exercise 7.1

LOOKUP exercises

1. In a new workbook enter the information below.

	A	B	C
1	**Product number**	**Name**	**Price**
2	C065	Mouse mat	£4.99
3	C123	Poster	£2.50
4	C157	Mug	£5.99
5	C232	Six greetings cards	£4.50
6	C306	Tea towel	£5.99

Define the area from A2 to C6 as **items**.

In cell B8 enter =VLOOKUP(A8,items,2) Now if you type a product number in A8, the product name will appear in B8.

Create another lookup so that the product's price (formatted to currency) appears in C8. Save the workbook as **Items.xls.**
Check the lookups work for all possible values.

2. Investigate what happens if you type in a false product number in this workbook.

(a) Try one that is too big like C350.

(b) Try one that is too small like C050.

(c) Try one that doesn't exist like C150.

3. Reopen the **Postage1.xls** workbook and switch to Sheet1. Set up a combo box linked to cell B13 as shown below and use VLOOKUP in cells C13, D13 and E13 to find the price of postage to each zone.

	A	B	C	D	E
1	No	Max weight (g)	Europe	World Zone 1	World Zone 2
2	1	100	£0.87	£1.15	£1.15
3	2	120	£0.96	£1.32	£1.34
4	3	140	£1.05	£1.49	£1.53
5	4	160	£1.14	£1.66	£1.72
6	5	180	£1.23	£1.83	£1.91
7	6	200	£1.32	£2.00	£2.10
8					
9					
10		Weight	180 ▼		
11					
12			Europe	World Zone 1	World Zone 2
13		5	£1.23	£1.83	£1.91

Hint
■ The formula in cell C13 will be =VLOOKUP(B13,weight,3) .

4. Using VLOOKUP, set up two combo boxes to choose the weight and the zone so that the cost of postage appears in a cell as shown below.

	A	B	C	D
18	1	Europe		
19	2	World Zone 1		
20	3	World Zone 2		
21				
22		Weight	100 ▼	World Zone 1 ▼
23				
24		1	2	£1.15

Hints
■ You will need to set up a new table first as shown.

■ Link the combo boxes to cells B24 and C24

■ The formula in D24 is

  =VLOOKUP(B24, weight, C24+2)

•5. A gas company has a file on its customers part of which is shown here:

	A	B	C	D	E	F
1	Cust no	Name	Address1	Address2	Address3	Units
2	1251	Mr Bill Brown	1 Primrose View	Burton upon Trent	DE14 6RD	7315
3	1252	Ms Eileen Sands	2 Primrose View	Burton upon Trent	DE14 6RD	12934
4	1253	Miss Elizabeth Bird	3 Primrose View	Burton upon Trent	DE14 6RD	8091
5	1254	Mr Charles Bryant	4 Primrose View	Burton upon Trent	DE14 6RD	9060
6	1255	Miss Maria Chambers	5 Primrose View	Burton upon Trent	DE14 6RD	8450
7	1256	Mr Darren Foreman	6 Primrose View	Burton upon Trent	DE14 6RD	9124
8	1257	Mrs Olive Hassent	7 Primrose View	Burton upon Trent	DE14 6RD	5067
9	1258	Miss Katie Johnson	8 Primrose View	Burton upon Trent	DE14 6RD	9818
10	1259	Mr Quinton Harris	9 Primrose View	Burton upon Trent	DE14 6RD	7168

Gas costs 1.17p per KWh (unit).

The bill also includes an 8p per day standing charge and 5 per cent VAT.

(a) In a new workbook set up a spreadsheet with the information above. If you use the Drag Copy short cut it will be much quicker. (See page 175).

(b) Use **Insert, Name, Define** to give the data a name.

(c) On Sheet 2 set up lookups so that if the customer number is typed in cell A2, the customer's name, address and units used appear like this:

	A	B	C	D	E
1	Cust no				
2	1256				
3					
4		Mr Darren Foreman		Units used	9124
5		6 Primrose View			
6		Burton upon Trent			
7		DE14 6RD			

(d) Check it works for at least four different customer numbers.

(e) Extend this sheet to calculate the whole bill as shown.

	A	B	C	D	E
1	Cust no			Start of period	01-Nov-00
2	1256			End of period	01-Feb-01
3					
4		Mr Darren Foreman		Units used	9124
5		6 Primrose View		Cost per unit	£0.0117
6		Burton upon Trent		Cost of gas	£106.75
7		DE14 6RD			
8				No of days	92
9				Standing charge per day	£0.08
10				Standing charge	£7.36
11					
12				Total	£114.11
13					
14				VAT	£5.71
15					
16				Total with VAT	£119.82

(f) Save the workbook as **Gas.xls**

As you enter different customer numbers, the bill will change.

Hint

- Use the following function in E8 to work out the number of days =DATEDIF(E1,E2,"D")

- Use the Increase Decimal icon on E5 to format the cell to 4 decimal places.

Option buttons and check boxes

In this section you will learn how to set up and use Option Buttons and Check Boxes.

Option buttons allow you to select one from a group of options. Option buttons are used when only one of several possibilities is allowed.

▶ WORKED EXAMPLE: How to set up an Option Button

1. Turn on the Forms toolbar:
    View, Toolbars, Forms.

2. Click on the **Option Button** icon.

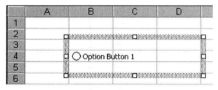

3. Drag out a rectangle on the worksheet. It will look like this:

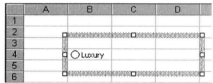

4. Highlight the text next to the button and enter the text Luxury.

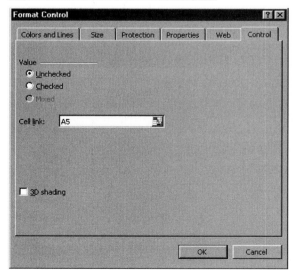

5. Right click on the control and use **Format Control** to set a cell link to A5.

6. Add three more option buttons in the same way.
   You will notice that they all are linked to the same cell.

Remember

■ If you want more than one group of option buttons on a worksheet, you will need to group them with a Group Box.

	A	B	C	D
1				
2				
3				
4		◯ Luxury		
5				
6				
7		◯ Standard		
8				
9				
10		◯ Economy		
11				
12				
13		◯ Basic		
14				
15				

7. When you click on a button, it changes the value in the linked cell.

Hint

■ To get all the buttons exactly in line, turn on the **Drawing** toolbar. Click on the **Select Objects** pointer tool and drag across all four option button boxes. Then click on **Draw, Align or Distribute, Align Left**. Remember to unselect the pointer

	A	B
1		
2		
3		
4		⦿ Luxury
5	1	
6		
7		◯ Standard
8		
9		
10		◯ Economy
11		
12		
13		◯ Basic

	A	B
1		
2		
3		
4		◯ Luxury
5	2	
6		
7		⦿ Standard
8		
9		
10		◯ Economy
11		
12		
13		◯ Basic

A carpet shop offers different quality carpets at different prices as shown on below left.

	A	B	C
1	Code	Type of carpet	Price/sq m
2	1	Luxury	£15.99
3	2	Standard	£12.99
4	3	Economy	£9.99
5	4	Basic	£5.99

8. Set up the option buttons shown on the previous page if you have not already done so.

9. On Sheet2 enter the prices. Highlight the cells from A2 to C5 and name them **prices** with **Insert, Name, Define**

10. Go back to Sheet1 and in cell E4 type in `=VLOOKUP(A5,prices,3)` .

	A	B	C	D	E
1					
2					
3					
4		○ Luxury			£ 9.99
5					
6					
7		○ Standard		Sq metres	12
8					
9					
10		◉ Economy			£ 119.88
11					
12					
13		○ Basic			

11. Check that as you click on a different option button the price in cell E4 changes.

12. Change the colour of the text in A5 to white so that it does not show.

13. Set up the spreadsheet to have a cell for the number of square metres and another cell to calculate the cost of the carpet as shown on the left.

14. Check it works for all four types of carpet.

Save your file as **Carpet.xls**.

■ Check boxes

A **check box** allows you turn an option on or off

▶ WORKED EXAMPLE: How to set up a Check box

We will use a check box to show whether the customer wishes to pay for fitting the carpet or not.

1. Load the spreadsheet **Carpet.xls** from the last exercise if it is not already loaded.

2. Turn on the Forms toolbar: **View, Toolbars, Forms**.

3. Click on the **Check Box** icon

4. Drag out a rectangle on the worksheet near cell B16.
   It will look like this:

12	
13	○ Basic
14	
15	
16	☐ Check Box 5
17	
18	

5. Highlight the text next to the box and enter the text Fitting

☐ Fitting

6. Right click on the control and use **Format Control** to set a cell link to A15.

7. As you tick the check box the linked cell changes from TRUE to FALSE.

8. Fitting costs £25. In cell E16 type in   =IF(A15=FALSE,0,25)

9. Test it works and format the cell to currency.

10. Add the contents of cells E10 and E16 in cell E19.

11. We don't want the words TRUE and FALSE to show, so change the colour of their text to white.

The worksheet now looks like this:

	A	B	C	D	E
1					
2					
3					
4		○ Luxury			£ 9.99
5					
6					
7		○ Standard		Sq metres	12
8					
9					
10		⊙ Economy			£ 119.88
11					
12					
13		○ Basic			
14					
15					
16		☑ Fitting			£ 25.00
17					
18					
19					£ 144.88

As you check and uncheck the boxes, the amounts will change.

12. Remove the gridlines, add a company name and format the text appropriately.

Save your file.

Spinners and scroll bars

In this section you will learn how to set up and use spinner controls and scroll bars.

A **spinner** or spin button is a button that enables you to increase or decrease the value of a number in a cell by clicking on the control

■ How to add a spinner

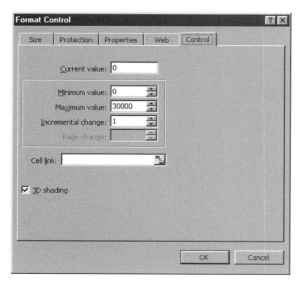

1. Turn on the Forms toolbar:
   View, Toolbars, Forms

2. Click on the **Spinner** icon

3. Drag out a rectangle in a cell on the worksheet. If you hold down the ALT key it will lock the control to the gridlines

4. Right click and use **Format Control** to link the control to a cell

When you link the spinner to a cell, you have to specify maximum and minimum values and the incremental change every time you click on the spinner.

↗ All the values must be whole numbers.

↗ The minimum value cannot be negative.

↗ The maximum value cannot be more than 30,000.

> ## A WORKED EXAMPLE: Share prices

The following steps show you how to add a spinner to a spreadsheet
used to store details of share prices and profits made.

	A	B	C	D	E	F	G	H	I
1									
2	Company	Number		Purchase	Current		Profit	Total	% Profit
3		held		price	price		per share	profit	
4	Rolls Royce	150		£ 1.50	£ 2.00				
5	PowerGen	200		£ 2.68	£ 2.00				
6	NatGrid	300		£ 1.54	£ 2.00				
7	RailTrack	300		£ 2.30	£ 3.00				
8									
9							Sum of		
10							profit		

1. Enter the row, column headings and data as shown above

2. In G4 enter the formula   `=E4-D4`

3. Copy the formula into G5, G6 and G7.

4. In H4 enter the formula   `=G4*B4`   (number of shares multiplied by
    profit per share).

5. Copy the formula into H5, H6 and H7.

6. In I4 enter the formula   `=G4/D4`
    Remember percentage profit is profit/purchase price.

7. Copy the formula into I5, I6 and I7.

8. Format column I as percentage.

9. Enter the formula   `=SUM(H4:H7)`   in H10.

    We will use a spinner to edit the number of shares.

10. Turn on the Forms toolbar **View, Toolbars,
    Forms**.

11. Click on the spinner icon and drag out a box
    in C4.

12. Right click on the control and click on
    Format Control.

13. Set the Maximum Value to 10000, the
    Minimum Value to 1 and the incremental
    change to 1.

14. Set the cell link to B4 and click **OK**

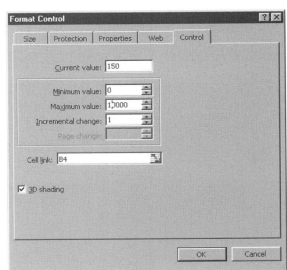

	A	B	C	D	E	F	G	H	I
1									
2	Company	Number		Purchase	Current		Profit	Total	% Profit
3		held		price	price		per share	profit	
4	Rolls Royce	150		£ 1.50	£ 2.00		£ 0.50	£ 75.00	33%
5	PowerGen	200		£ 2.68	£ 2.00		-£ 0.68	-£ 136.00	-25%
6	NatGrid	300		£ 1.54	£ 2.00		£ 0.46	£ 138.00	30%
7	RailTrack	300		£ 2.30	£ 3.00		£ 0.70	£ 210.00	30%
8									
9							Sum of		
10							profit	£ 287.00	

15. Repeat the process for spinners in cells C5, C6 and C7. Alternatively you can copy and paste the control to the remaining cells but remember to change the cell link. You may wish to insert rows to improve the layout.

Altering the current price of the shares alters the percentage profit. We will use a spinner to edit the current price.

16. Add a spinner to F4 linked to cell E4. Set the minimum and maximum values to 1 and 100, with the increment at 1.You will notice the value goes up by £1 at a time and clearly you need to be able to increase the price in pence

17. In K4 (somewhere off screen) enter 200 and link the spinner in F4 to K4 by going back to **Format Control**. Change also the maximum value to 2000.

18. In E4 enter the formula =K4/100

19. The spinner should now increment in pence. You can hide the contents of cell F4 by using the tip on page 181.

20. You should now be able to complete the task and update the spreadsheet with the latest share prices

Save your file as **Shares.xls**

> **Note**
> ■ Even when a cell has a spinner attached, you can still type a value into the cell

Spinner exercise

Exercise 9.1

Load the file **Gas.xls** from Unit 7. Add a spinner to Sheet2 to increase and decrease the customer number by 1 so that you can cycle through all the records in the file.

■ Scroll bars

A **scroll bar** enables you to increase or decrease the value in a cell by
clicking the control or dragging the slide bar

■ How to add a scroll bar

1. Turn on the Forms toolbar: **View**, **Toolbars**,
   Forms.

2. Click on the **Scroll Bar** icon.

3. Drag out a rectangle in a cell on the
   worksheet.

4. Right click and use **Format Control** to link
   the control to a cell.

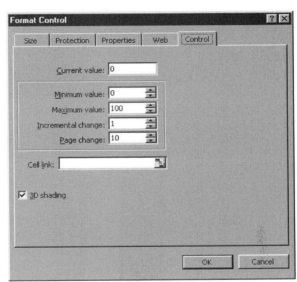

When you link the scroll bar to a cell, you have
to specify maximum and minimum values and
the incremental change every time you click on
the scroll bar.

◢ All the values must be whole numbers.

◢ The minimum value cannot be negative.

◢ The maximum value cannot be more than
   30,000.

◢ You can choose whether or not to print
   spinners and scroll bars by right clicking on the control, clicking
   on **Format Control** and then clicking on the **Properties** tab.
   Check the **Print object** box.

◢ The page change refers to the size of the change if you click on the
   scroll bar itself rather than on one of the arrows.

> ### A WORKED EXAMPLE: A loan repayment calculator

	A	B	C	D
1				
2		Price of Car	£10,000.00	
3		Down Payment	£5,000.00	
4		Loan		
5		Interest rate	10%	
6		Years	3	
7		Payment		
8				
9				

1. Enter the row headings and data as shown above.

2. In C4 enter the formula =C2–C3

3. In C7 enter the formula =PMT(C5/12,C6*12,C4)
   For more details on this function, see later in this unit.

4. Turn on the Forms toolbar: **View, Toolbars, Forms**.

5. Click on the **Scroll Bar** icon and drag out a rectangle in D3.

6. Right click on the control and click **Format Control**.

7. Set the maximum and minimum values to 10000 and 0 with the increment at 100.

8. Link the **Scroll bar** to cell C3.

9. Set the page change to 1000.

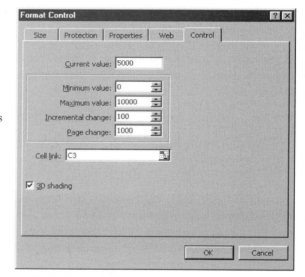

10. Put a scroll bar in D6 linked to cell C6 and set the maximum and minimum values to 5 and 1 with an increment of 1.

Your finished spreadsheet should appear as below:

Save your file as **Loans.xls**.

	A	B	C	D	E
1					
2		Price of Car	£10,000.00		
3		Down Payment	£5,000.00	◄ ▶	
4		Loan	£5,000.00		
5		Interest rate	10%		
6		Years	3	◄ ▶	
7		Payment	-£161.34		
8					
9					

Further development

We have seen that spinners and scroll bars only increment in whole numbers and you have also seen a way around it.

Interest rates usually increment by one decimal place and down payments are often quoted as a percentage.

1. Add scroll bars for the interest rate
2. Edit the scroll bar for the down payment to quote as a percentage of the car price

Financial functions

Excel has many built in functions. The **PMT** function is a financial function that calculates the repayments for a loan based on the interest rate, the number of payments and the amount borrowed.

There are many other financial functions available in Excel. Use Help to investigate further.

The **Future Value** and **Rate** functions are two of the more commonly used.

The Future Value (FV) function

This function returns the **Future value** of an investment assuming constant periodic payments and a constant interest rate.

Suppose you invest £100 per month for 2 years at 5% interest per annum.

The formula to calculate the value of your money after 2 years is:
`=FV(5%/12,24,-100)`

- 5% is the interest rate.
- 24 is the number of payments.
- -100 means a monthly payment of £100. It is negative because it is a payment.

The Rate function

The **Rate** function works out the interest rate given the amount borrowed, the number of payments and the amount of each payment.

The formula `=RATE(24,-230,5000)` works out the interest rate for a loan of £5 000, repaid at £230 a month for 24 months.

The result is **0.81%.**

(If your computer gives this as 1%, click on the **Increase decimal** icon.)

However this is the monthly interest rate. Multiply by 12 for the annual interest rate. The formula would be `=RATE(24,-230,5000)*12`

The result is **9.7%.**

Macros

In this section, you will learn how to speed up commonly used actions using:

 macros;

 macro buttons;

 customised icons to run macros.

■ Introduction

A **macro** is a program that stores a series of Microsoft Excel commands so that they can be executed as a single command.

There are two ways to create a macro in Excel:

 write the macro in Visual Basic or

 record the macro.

Recording the macro is much easier than writing it in Visual Basic.

▶ WORKED EXAMPLE 1:   A Macro to set the page to landscape

Always work through the macro steps before recording them.

In this example the steps are click **File, Page Setup**, check **Landscape** and click **OK**

Recording the macro

We will use the workbook called **Accounts** that we set up in Unit 2.

1. Load the file called **Accounts.xls**.

2. Click on **Tools, Macro, Record New Macro**.

3. Change the name of the macro to **Landscape**.

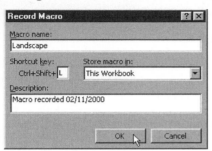

4. Press SHIFT + L to assign a **Shortcut key** to the macro and in the **Description box** give some brief details of your macro, by default it will display the date of recording.

   N.B. Excel uses many CTRL shortcut keys so always use CTRL and SHIFT to avoid replacing the defaults.

5. Store the macro in **This Workbook** and click **OK**. This toolbar appears on the screen.

6. Click on **File, Page Setup**. From the **Page** tab check **Landscape** and click on **OK**.

7. Click on the **Stop Recording** icon or click **Tools, Macro, Stop Recording**.

Testing the macro

We now need to test the macro works.

Set the page to portrait and click on **Tools, Macro, Macros, Landscape, Run**.

The screen will flicker. To test that the macro has operated correctly, check that the page is now set to landscape by clicking on **File, Page Setup**.

NB The shortcut ALT + F8 is useful for running macros.
Remember to save your file.

Exercise 10.1

Macro exercise 1: Setting the page to portrait

1. Record another macro called **Portrait** to switch the page to portrait.

Save your file again.

WORKED EXAMPLE 2:   Switching to another worksheet

We will record a macro called **ICT** to switch to the ICT worksheet using the file Accounts.

This may not seem very useful because you could just use the sheet tabs but eventually they will be removed.

1. Make sure that you select a different worksheet (not ICT) to start with.

2. Click on **Tools, Macro, Record New Macro** and call the new macro **ICT**.

3. Click on the **ICT** Sheet tab.

4. Click on **Stop Recording**.

Macro exercise 2: Switching to other sheets

Exercise 10.2

1. Record three more macros called Food, Design and Summary, each one to load a different worksheet of this workbook.

Viewing the macro coding

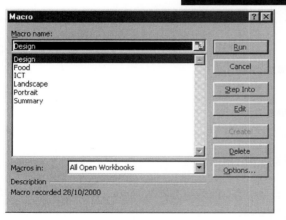

If you want to see what the Visual Basic coding of the recorded macro looks like, click on **Tools, Macro, Macros...**

Click on the name **Design** and then **Edit**. The Visual Basic Editor will load. (We will look at the Visual Basic Editor later in more detail. See page 72.)

On the right of the screen is the main Visual Basic Editor window, where the coding of the macro will be displayed as follows.

```
Sub Design()
`
`  Design Macro
`  Macro recorded 28/10/2000
`


`
     Sheets("Design").Select
End Sub
```

- The first line is the name of the macro. All macros begin with **Sub**.

- The next five lines in green are just information about the macro. They do not affect its behaviour.

- The next line is the operation you have recorded.

- The last line is the end of the macro. All macros end in **End Sub**.

- This is a very short macro. The Landscape macro, for example, is much longer. Scroll up if you want to view it.

Editing a macro

It is unlikely that you will want to edit this macro, but you can do so simply by editing the text. For example, you could change

```
Sheets("Design").Select   into
Sheets("ICT").Select
```

To go back to Excel click on the **View Microsoft Excel** icon or click on **View, Microsoft Excel**.

N.B. It is quicker to use ALT + F11.

▶ WORKED EXAMPLE 3: Removing the gridlines from the screen

We often want to remove the gridlines from the screen so that it does not look like a spreadsheet.

1. Click on **Tools, Macro, Record New Macro** and call the new macro **GridOff**. (You cannot have spaces in a macro name).

2. Click on **Tools, Options** and click on the **View** tab. Uncheck the **Gridlines** box. Click on **OK**.

3. Click on **Stop Recording**.

Exercise 10.3

▶ Macro exercise 3: A macro to turn the gridlines on

1. Record a macro called **GridOn** to put back the gridlines.

2. Test both your new macros.

Using buttons to Run Macros

To run a macro, we must click on **Tools, Macro, Macros**... We then click on the name of the macro and then click on **Run**.

This involves five mouse actions. By setting up a button we can cut this down to one action simply clicking on a button.

1. Load the file **Accounts.xls** if it is not already loaded. Select the Faculty Summary worksheet.

2. Turn on the Forms toolbar by clicking on **View, Toolbars, Forms**

3. Click on the **Button** icon and drag out a button near the bottom of the worksheet. (To align the button with the gridlines, hold the ALT key down as you drag.) You will see this box below:

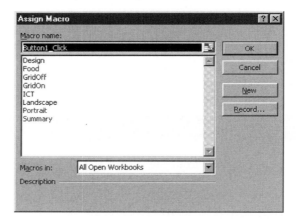

4. Click on the **GridOff** macro and click on **OK**

5. Click on the button to rename the text on the button.

We have now combined several operations into one click of the mouse.

6. Add another button to run the **GridOn** macro.

> **Note**
> - Right click on the button or use CTRL and click to select it so that you can move it, resize it, edit the text or assign a different macro.
> - Although a button appears on a worksheet and moves with the worksheet as you scroll up and down, it will not print.

Macro exercise 4: Adding buttons

1. Set up buttons on the Faculty Summary worksheet to run the **Landscape** and **Portrait** macros.

2. Set up buttons on the Faculty Summary worksheet to run the **ICT**, **Food** and **Design** macros.

3. Test all your buttons. Your finished sheet should appear as below.

4. Save your file.

	A	B	C	D	E	F	G	H	I	J
1										
2					Faculty of Technology Accounts 2000/2001					
3			Equipment	Software	Text Books	Stationery	Reprographics	Repairs	Total	Budget
4										
5		ICT	£ 550.00	£ 300.00	£ 500.00	£ 500.00	£ 600.00	£0.00	£2,450.00	£ 4,500.00
6		Food	£ 200.00	£ 200.00	£ 450.00	£ 400.00	£ 300.00	£ 250.00	£1,800.00	£ 3,400.00
7		Design	£ 1,500.00	£ 200.00	£ 800.00	£ 300.00	£ 400.00	£ 700.00	£3,900.00	£ 5,500.00
8										
9		Total	£ 2,250.00	£ 700.00	£ 1,750.00	£1,200.00	£ 1,300.00	£ 950.00	£8,150.00	£ 13,400.00
10										
11		Landscape		Portrait		Food		Design		ICT
12										

Designing your own buttons

You don't have to click on a button to run a macro. You could click on a picture instead. It could be a picture you have designed yourself, one from clip-art, an Excel **AutoShape** or even **WordArt**.

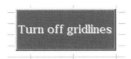

Turn off gridlines

1. Turn on the Drawing toolbar with **View**, **Toolbars**, **Drawing**.

2. Click on **AutoShapes**. Click on **Basic Shapes** on the menu and choose a shape such as a **Rectangle**.

3. Drag out a rectangle on the screen.

4. Right click on your shape. Click on **Format AutoShape** and choose a colour using the **Colors and Lines** tab.

5. Right click on the shape again and click on **Add Text**. Type in the text and change colour, font and size in the normal way.

6. Right click on the shape again and click on **Assign Macro**. Click on the name of the macro you want to run.

Setting up an icon to run a macro

Buttons are very useful for running macros, but they will not be on the screen if you scroll down or choose another worksheet. Another way of running a macro is to set up an icon on a toolbar.

> **Note**
>
> **Warning:**
> - Some networks restrict whether you can alter the settings. If you edit the toolbars to include new icons, these may not be there when you next log on.
> - It is a good idea to see if you can save your icons as you don't want to spend a lot of time setting up icons that won't save.

Suppose we want to add an icon to the Standard Toolbar to run the macro called **GridOff**. We will use the **Accounts.xls** file again.

1. Click on **View, Toolbars, Customize.**
   The box on the left appears:

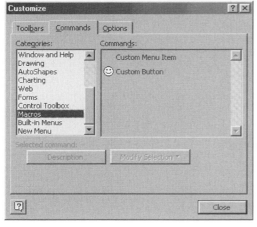

2. Click on the **Commands** tab and scroll down in the list until you see **Macros** and click on it.
   A smiley face appears in the Commands box.

3. Drag the smiley face icon on to the Standard Toolbar where you want the new icon and let go.

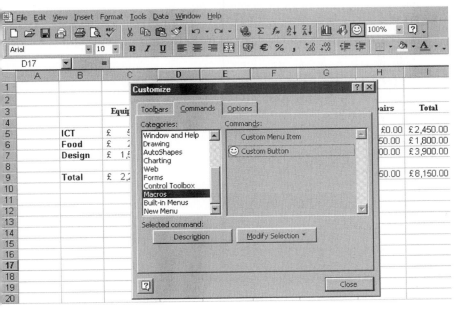

4. Right click on the smiley face icon.

5. Click on **Change Button Image** to have a selection of possible icons.

6. Right click on the icon again and click on **Edit Button Image** to load a simple painting program to edit your icon.

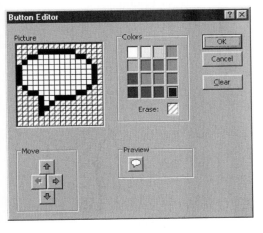

7. Edit your icon as you think suitable.

8. Right click on the icon again, click on **Assign Macro** and choose the Grid Off macro.

9. Click on **Close** on the main dialogue box.

Test that the new icon works.

Note

- You can also use this method to edit existing icons, for example to change the colour scheme on them.
- You can add icons and text to the drop-down menus in exactly the same way.
- To remove the icon. Right click on it, select **Customize** and drag the icon onto the **Customize window**

Exercise 10.5

Macro exercise 5

Set up an icon on the same toolbar to run the **GridOn** macro.

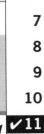

Further macros

In this section, you will learn how to use macros to perform common processing tasks in Excel.

> ▶ **WORKED EXAMPLE 1:   Setting up a macro to extend a named area**

1.   Enter the data below.

	A	B	C	D	E	F
1	**Surname**	**Forename**			Dolman	Martyn
2	Knott	Alan				
3	Parks	Jim				
4	Murray	John				
5	Russell	Jack				
6	Allman	Don				

2.   Highlight cells A1 to B6 and use **Insert, Name, Define** to name the area **namefile**.

We are going to extend the named area by one row, add a new name and sort it into alphabetical order.

3.   Enter the new surname into cell E1 and the new forename in cell F1.

4.   Start recording a macro by clicking **Tools, Macro, Record New Macro** and name it **Add**.

5.   Click on row heading 2 and click on **Insert, Rows**.

6.   Highlight cells E1 and F1 and click on the **Cut** icon.

7.   Click on cell A2 and click **Paste**.

8.   Click on **namefile** in the names box to select the named area.

9.   Click on **Data, Sort**. Make sure the Header row button is checked. Sort by **Surname, Ascending**. Click **OK** and click off the area to remove the highlighting.

	A	B
1	**Surname**	**Forename**
2	Allman	Don
3	Dolman	Martyn
4	Knott	Alan
5	Murray	John
6	Parks	Jim
7	Russell	Jack

10. Stop recording and test the macro for two or three more names. The file should appear as above.

▶

> ▶ **Further macros exercise 1**
>
> Record a macro to delete a record from the named area. You will need to select the row to be deleted before recording the macro.

Exercise 11.1

▶ WORKED EXAMPLE 2:   Updating sales

A shop stores details of the number of items in stock and today's sales.

	A	B	C
1		No in stock	Today's Sales
2	Corn Flakes	179	41

Every time the shop sells a packet of Corn Flakes, the number in C2 increases by one.

We will set up a macro to automate this procedure.

◻ What will the macro do?

The macro will add one to the number in C2 (41) and put the answer in D2. This will then be copied into C2 and D2 will be cleared.

◻ Recording the macro

1. Set up the cells as shown.
2. Click on **Tools, Macro, Record New Macro**.
3. Call the macro **AddOne** and set up the short cut key as CTRL + SHIFT +M.
4. Click on cell D2.
5. Enter the formula `=C2+1`
6. Click on cell D2 again and select the **Copy** icon
7. Click on cell C2 and click on **Edit, Paste Special, Values, OK**.
8. Click on cell D2 again and select **Edit, Clear, All**.
9. Stop recording.
10. Check that if you press CTRL + SHIFT +M, the number in C2 increases by 1.

11. Set up a button over cell D2 to run this macro.

12. Save the file as **Update.xls**.

▶ WORKED EXAMPLE 3:   Updating stock levels

At the end of each day, the shopkeeper needs to update the stock levels, to see the new stock level and find out if any new stock needs to be ordered.

	A	B	C
1		No in stock	Today's Sales
2	Corn Flakes	179	41

What will the macro do?

The macro will take the number in C2 (41) away from the number in B2 (179.) The answer (138) will be in a different cell, E2. This will then be copied into B2. C2 will then be reset to zero and E2 will be cleared.

Recording the macro

We can record a macro to do the updating automatically as follows:

1. Click on **Tools, Macro, Record New Macro.** Change the name of the macro to **Update**.

2. Click on cell E2 and type in the formula =B2 – C2   Press ENTER. *(This works out the new number in stock.)*

3. Click on cell E2 again and click on **Edit**, **Copy**.

4. Click on cell B2 and click on **Edit, Paste Special, Values** and click on **OK** *(The new number in stock is now in B2.)*

5. Click on cell C2 and type in **0**. Press ENTER

6. Click on cell E2 and click on **Edit, Clear, All**.

7. Click on **Stop Recording**.

8. Set up a button over cell F2 to run the Update macro.

Testing the macro

9. Type a new figure for today's sales in C2.

10. Run the Update macro.

Test that the number in stock has been updated correctly. Save the file.

WORKED EXAMPLE 4:

	A	B	C	D	E	F
1	Title	Forename	Surname	Address	Town	Postcode
2	Mrs	Margaret	Fisher	204 Meadow Road	Burton upon Trent	DE13 0LL
3	Ms	Jennifer	Adcock	23 The Weeping	Derby	DE9 3SK
4	Mrs	Margaret	Thompson	72 Wood Field Road	Burton upon Trent	DE14 5RT
5	Mrs	Kerry	Brown	3 Manor Farm Crescent	Matlock	DE35 9UJ
6	Mrs	Maggie	Crame	3 Blackbird View	Derby	DE2 6UJ
7	Mrs	Elaine	Patel	6 Yak Sq	Burton upon Trent	DE13 5RF
8	Mrs	Jean	Freeman	2 Trent Ave	Derby	DE2 9UH
9	Mr	Imran	Hussein	41 Derby St	Burton upon Trent	DE14 3ED
10	Mrs	Jackie	Noble	2 Black Farm Road	Derby	DE3 4RF
11	Mrs	Niru	Najib	6 Jackson Close	Burton upon Trent	DE12 9PP
12	Mr	Colin	White	56 Norton Villa	Burton upon Trent	DE14 7GV

	A	B	C	D	E	F
1	Title	Forename	Surname	Address	Town	Postcode
2	Mr	Oliver	Blake	5 Swallow Walk	Burton upon Trent	DE17 8AZ
3	Mrs	Linda	Butler	5 George Street	Matlock	DE35 7KI
4	Mrs	Elaine	Sands	113 High St	London	NW12 2ER
5	Mrs	Fiona	Calder	12c Le Grand Rise	Burton upon Trent	DE14 7YT
6	Mr	Mark	Harvey	45 Maxton Street	Derby	DE4 8UH

A company keeps a record of its clients in a worksheet called **Customers.**

They also store details of former customers in a worksheet called **Old Customers**.

Whenever a customer closes their account, the data is not deleted but transferred from the **Customers** worksheet to the **Old Customers** worksheet, in case it is needed in future.

This is another frequently performed task and so should be performed by a macro.

1. Enter the above data into worksheets Sheet2 and Sheet3 and rename the worksheets **Customers** and **Old Customers**.

2. Select the **Customers** worksheet.

3. Highlight one of the records, e.g. all the details for Mrs Kerry Brown. (Cells A5 to F5).

4. Click on **Tools, Macro, Record New Macro.** Call the macro **Old** and click on **OK**.

5. Click on the **Cut** icon.

6. Click on the **Old Customers** worksheet tab.

7. Select cell A2.

8. Click on **Insert, Cut Cells**

9. Click on **Shift cells down**.

The record for Mrs Kerry Brown has now been inserted in the **Old Customers** worksheet.

	A	B	C	D	E	F
1	Title	Forename	Surname	Address	Town	Postcode
2	Mrs	Kerry	Brown	3 Manor Farm Cres	Matlock	DE35 9UJ
3	Mr	Oliver	Blake	5 Swallow Walk	Burton upon Trent	DE17 8AZ
4	Mrs	Linda	Butler	5 George Street	Matlock	DE35 7KI
5	Mrs	Elaine	Sands	113 High St	London	NW12 2ER
6	Mrs	Fiona	Calder	12c Le Grand Rise	Burton upon Trent	DE14 7YT
7	Mr	Mark	Harvey	45 Maxton Street	Derby	DE4 8UH

10. Click on the **Customers** worksheet tab.

11. Click on **Edit, Delete**. Click on **Shift cells up**.

12. Click on **Stop Recording**.

13. Save the file as **Clients.xls**.

14. Highlight another customer on the **Customers** worksheet and test the macro.

Exercise 11.2

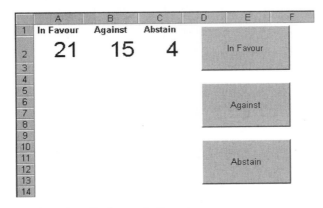

Further macros exercise 2

1. A former customer has reopened their account. Record a second macro called **Reopen** to transfer a highlighted record from the **Old Customers** worksheet to the **Customers** worksheet.

2. Shops stock more than one product. Enter at least four more products into Sheet1 like this.

	A	B	C
1		No in stock	Today's Sales
2	Corn Flakes	56	12
3	Baked Beans	199	34
4	Tea bags	510	134
5	Instant coffee	23	2
6	Brown sauce	32	15

   Record a macro called **Update2** to update all stock levels for all the products.

3. The US Senate is considering an electronic voting system for the 100 senators. When they vote, they will simply click a button on a screen that looks like this.

	A	B	C	D	E	F
1	In Favour	Against	Abstain			
2	21	15	4		In Favour	
3						
4						
5						
6					Against	
7						
8						
9						
10						
11					Abstain	
12						
13						
14						

The computer automatically counts the votes.

Set up a system with three macros, so that each time you click on the button the appropriate number increases by one. Save the system as **Senate.xls**.

How to make your macro available whenever you use Excel

Normally a macro is stored in the workbook. It is only available if that particular workbook is open.

If you want your macro to be available whenever you load Excel, store it in the **Personal Workbook.**

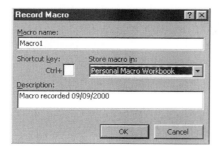

This can be done as follows:

1. Click on **Tools, Macro, Record New Macro**.

2. Click on **Store macro in Personal Macro Workbook**.

The macro is stored in a file called Personal.xls.

If you wish to edit this macro, you will need to click on **Window, Unhide, Personal.xls**. This opens the Personal.xls workbook.

The Security Message

This message appears when you open an Excel file with macros stored in it. It is a protection against viruses that may be stored in macros from an unreliable source.

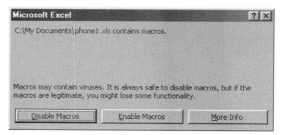

Click on **Enable Macros** or the macros will not work.

You can disable this warning by clicking on **Tools, Macro, Security**

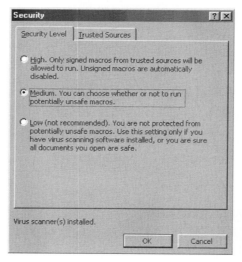

Click on **Low** security. This may not be recommended but is alright if you have written the macros.

In Excel 97 click on **Tools, Options**. Select the **General** tab and uncheck **Macro Virus Protection**.

Customising the screen

In this section, we will look at how to adapt the screen when your system loads using

◢ the **auto_open macro**

◢ the **auto_close macro**

The display on the screen must be as user-friendly as possible. When designing a spreadsheet you must think of the needs of the user. We have already seen that you can set up macros to remove or replace the gridlines.

◢ Do they want to display the row and column headings?

◢ Do you need the sheet tabs?

◢ What colour should the text and background be?

Using macros and **Tools, Options, View** you can customise the screen exactly to the users' requirements.

See Customising your screen output, page 186.

The Auto_Open Macro

The Auto_Open macro is a special macro that runs when you load an Excel file.

For example you could use it to:

◢ set the font;

◢ set the font colour;

◢ set the background colour;

◢ turn on or off some of the toolbars;

◢ remove the worksheet tabs;

◢ remove the status bar at the bottom of the screen;

◢ remove the formula bar;

◢ remove the scroll bars;

◢ remove the gridlines;

◢ remove the row and column headings.

■ There is another macro called the **Auto_Close** macro, which runs when you close a file. You could use this to put back the controls when you exit from the file.

■ It is possible to disable the **Auto_Open** macro so that it does not run when the file has been loaded. Simply hold down the SHIFT key while the file is loading.

Further macros exercise 3:

1. Load the file **Accounts.xls** and record a macro called **Auto_Open** to remove the tabs, scroll bars, row and column headings, the gridlines, the status bar and the formula bar.

2. Record another macro called **Auto_Close** to put them all back.
   Test the macros work when you open the file and close it

   The coding of the **Auto_Open** and **Auto_Close** macros will be as follows:

```
Sub auto_open()
   With ActiveWindow
      .DisplayGridlines = False
      .DisplayHeadings = False
      .DisplayHorizontalScrollBar = False
      .DisplayVerticalScrollBar = False
      .DisplayWorkbookTabs = False
   End With

With Application
      .DisplayFormulaBar = False
      .DisplayStatusBar = False
   End With
End Sub

Sub auto_close()
   With ActiveWindow
      .DisplayGridlines = True
      .DisplayHeadings = True
      .DisplayHorizontalScrollBar = True
      .DisplayVerticalScrollBar = True
      .DisplayWorkbookTabs = True
   End With
   With Application
      .DisplayFormulaBar = True
      .DisplayStatusBar = True
   End With
End Sub
```

3. Click on **Tools, Macro, Macros, GridOff, Edit** and underneath the coding type this in:

```
Sub GridToggle()
    mygrid = ActiveWindow.DisplayGridlines
    ActiveWindow.DisplayGridlines = Not mygrid
End Sub
```

4. Set up a button to run this macro.

This macro **GridToggle** toggles the gridlines, i.e. run it once to remove the gridlines. Run it again to put them back. The second line reads the old value – are the gridlines on or off? The third line sets the new value to the opposite of the old value.

5. Set up a macro called **TabsToggle** to toggle the worksheet tabs on and off.

The Visual Basic Editor

In this section you will learn at how to use the Visual Basic Editor to customise certain features in Excel.

The use of Visual Basic is not usually within the spirit of ICT specifications. The chosen software package should drive the solution and not Visual Basic code. However you can use a little code to enhance your solution.

■ Introduction

The Visual Basic Editor Window is used for entering commands in Excel's programming language Visual Basic.

Although you do not need to know anything about Visual Basic to record a macro, you need to know a little about Visual Basic if you want to do things such as:

◢ editing macros recorded in Microsoft Excel;

◢ setting up message boxes and input boxes;

◢ setting up UserForms.

To work in Visual Basic, load the **Visual Basic Editor**.

1. Load the file Accounts.xls from Unit 10.

2. Click on **Tools, Macro, Visual Basic Editor** or press ALT + **F11**.

There are three parts to the **Visual Basic Editor**, the **Project Explorer Window**, the **Properties Window** and the **Visual Basic Editor Window.**

Make sure that the **Project Explorer** and the **Properties Window** are on the screen.

If they are turned off click on **View, Project Explorer** and **View, Properties Window**.

Adjust the size of the windows and move them by dragging in the normal way so that they are in the positions shown in the picture.

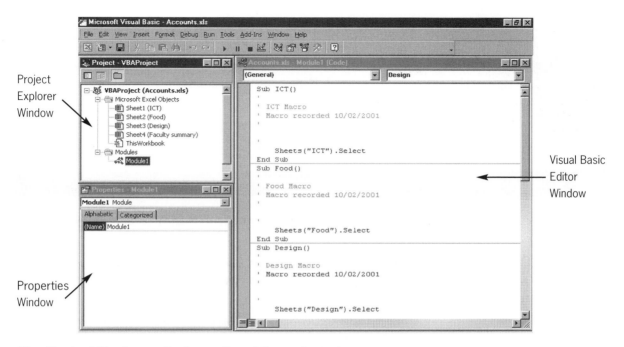

Project Explorer Window

Properties Window

Visual Basic Editor Window

The Project Explorer displays a list of the projects. Any open workbook is a project consisting of worksheets, modules (where macros and other Visual Basic code is stored) and UserForms.

If you double click on **Module1.** The coding for all the macros stored in Module 1 will appear in the main Visual Basic Editor window.

■ Why is there sometimes a Module1 and a Module2?

If you record several macros in one session they will be stored in Module1. If later in another session, you record some more macros, they will be stored in Module 2 and so on. It will not affect the user if a macro is stored in Module1 or Module2.

The **Properties Window** displays the properties for the objects that make up the project, e.g. UserForms, Worksheets, etc.

With just a little knowledge of Visual Basic it is possible to start customising your systems. The next section uses a little Visual Basic to introduce Message Boxes.

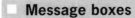

Message boxes

A message box is a small dialog box that displays information and requests an action. An example appears below, a helpline number is given and the user clicks OK.

Setting up a message box involves one command in Microsoft Visual Basic.

WORKED EXAMPLE 1: A Simple Information Message box

1. Click **Tools, Macro, Visual Basic Editor** to load the Visual Basic Editor.

2. Double click on Module1 in the Project Explorer window. (If Module1 does not appear in the **Project Explorer** window, click on **Insert, Module**).

3. Scroll down to the bottom of the macro coding in the main Visual Basic Editor window.

4. Enter this text to set up a macro called Message1:

```
Sub Message1()
MsgBox "Our helpline is 0208 341 3411.", vbOKOnly, "LPX Mobile"
End Sub
```

> **Note**
> - As with recorded macros, the macro must begin with Sub and end with End Sub.
> - You will not need to type in the **End Sub** part as when you enter a line beginning with Sub, the End Sub line is automatically inserted below.
> - You can define the title, the message and the buttons.
> - vbOKOnly means you get just an OK button.

5. Go back to Excel by clicking on the **View Microsoft Excel** icon.

6. Run the macro Message1 by clicking on **Tools, Macro, Macros, Message1, Run** and you will see the above message box.

WORKED EXAMPLE 2: Displaying options on a message box

We might want the user to make a choice from a message box.

Here is an example where the message box has a **Yes** button and a **No** button. Clicking on **Yes** exits from Excel. Clicking on **No** does nothing.

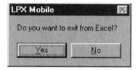

```
Sub quit()
Response = MsgBox("Do you want to exit from Excel?", vbYesNo, "LPX Mobile")
If Response = vbYes Then
     Application.Quit
Else
End If
End Sub
```

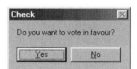

Message Box exercise 1

Exercise 12.1

1. Create a macro called *About* to set up a message box to say who created your system and give the date.

2. Set up a button to run the above macro.

3. In the last chapter on page 67 we looked at a system called **senate.xls** to computerise voting in the US Senate. Suppose a senator clicked the wrong button by mistake. By adding four lines at the start of each macro we can use a message box as a double check.

```
Response = MsgBox("Do you want to vote in favour?", vbYesNo, "Check")
If Response = vbNo Then
     End
End If
```

If the senator chooses yes, one is added to the counter. If the senator chooses no, nothing happens.

Edit all three macros in the system so that they have a message box to confirm the vote.

Some useful Message box settings

vbOKOnly   Displays the **OK** button only

vbOKCancel   Displays the **OK** and **Cancel** buttons.

vbAbortRetryIgnore Displays the **Abort**, **Retry**, and **Ignore** buttons.

vbYesNoCancel   Displays the **Yes**, **No**, and **Cancel** buttons.

vbYesNo   Displays the **Yes** and **No** buttons.

Message box icons

By adding an extra command, you can add one of four special icons to a message box. For example:

vbOKOnly + vbCritical displays the **OK** button and the **Critical Message** icon.

The command would look like this:

```
MsgBox "Created by C.A.Robins © 2001", vbOKOnly +
vbCritical, "Information"
```

Use vbCritical for the **Critical Message** icon.

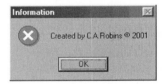

Use vbQuestion for the **Question Message** icon.

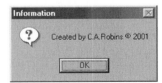

Use vbExclamation for the **Warning Message** icon.

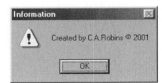

Use `vbInformation` for the **Information Message** icon.

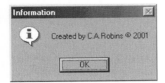

Message Box exercise 2

Exercise 12.2

1. Add the information message icon to the message box in Message Box exercise 1 question 1.

2. Add the warning query icon to the message boxes in Message Box exercise 1 question 3.

Input boxes

An input box is another on-screen dialogue box. You can use it to enter data and paste the data into a cell.

1. Load the **Visual Basic Editor** by clicking on **Tools, Macro, Visual Basic Editor**

2. Double click on Module1 in the Project Explorer window.

3. Scroll down to the bottom of the macro coding and type in this macro:

```
Sub ibox()
Dim value
Range("H3").Select
   value = InputBox ("How many minutes?", "LPX Mobile")
ActiveCell.value = value
End Sub
```

The macro does the following:

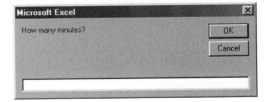

- sets up a variable called value;
- selects cell H3;
- loads this input box.
- Pastes the input data into cell H3.

Input box exercise

Exercise 12.3

1 Load the file from Unit 11 called **update.xls**. Set up a macro to display an input box. The input box asks 'How many packets of Corn Flakes have been delivered today?' The answer is pasted into cell F2.

Can you extend the macro so that the number delivered today in F2 is added to the number in stock in cell B2?

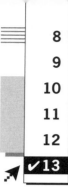
UserForms

In this section you will learn about UserForms and how they can be used as a user-friendly front end for an Excel workbook.

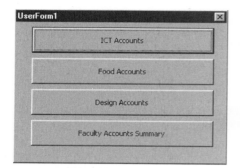

A UserForm is a way of providing a customised user-interface for your system. A simple UserForm might look like the one on the left:

Load the file **accounts.xls**

This file contains macros called ICT, Design, Food and Summary to switch between the different worksheets.

▶ WORKED EXAMPLE 1:   Setting up a Front End UserForm

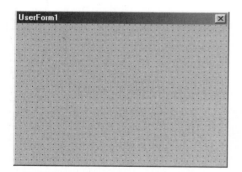

1. Load the **Visual Basic Editor** by clicking on **Tools, Macro, Visual Basic Editor**.

2. Click on **Insert, UserForm** or click on the Insert UserForm icon. A blank UserForm will appear in the main Visual Basic Editor window looking like this:

3. A set of icons called the Toolbox will also appear. If it is not visible, click on the blank UserForm and click on **View, Toolbox** (see below)

4. On the Toolbox, click on the Command Button icon and drag out a rectangle on the UserForm near the top.

5. The text on the button will say **CommandButton1**. Edit this by clicking once on the button. Delete and change to **ICT accounts**.

6. Double click on the button. You will see:

```
Private Sub CommandButton1_Click()

End Sub
```

The cursor should be in the middle of these two lines. If not, click between the two lines. Type this in:

```
ICT
UserForm1.Hide
```

It will now look like this:

```
Private Sub CommandButton1_Click()
ICT
UserForm1.Hide
End Sub
```

ICT is the name of the macro that will run when you click on this button.

The command `UserForm1.Hide` removes the UserForm from the screen.

7. Click on the **View Object** icon in the Project Explorer Window (top left of screen) to go back to the plan of the UserForm.

8. Add three more buttons to run the other three macros. The UserForm will now look like this:

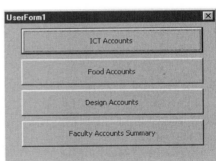

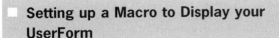

> ■ The spelling and the punctuation must be exactly as above or it won't work.
> ■ If when you are in the Visual Basic Editor, you insert a second UserForm by mistake, you can delete it by clicking on **File, Remove UserForm**

The UserForm is now set up. Save your file. Test the UserForm by clicking on the Run Sub/User Form icon or press F5.

The User Form will load. When you select a worksheet you will go back to the Visual Basic Editor.

Setting up a Macro to Display your UserForm

Once you have designed a UserForm, you will need to set up a macro to display it. The macro will be set up in Visual Basic and once again, exact syntax is vital.

1. In Excel, click on **Tools, Macro, Visual Basic Editor**.

2. Double click on Module1 in the Project Explorer window. (If Module1 is not visible click on the + sign next to **Modules** in the Project Explorer window. Then double click on Module1.)

3. You should see the coding of the macros you have already set up. Scroll down to the bottom and underneath the last macro text, type in the following:

```
Sub Box()
Load UserForm1
UserForm1.Show
End Sub
```

These two lines of code load the User Form and display it on the screen.

You will not need to type in the **End Sub** part as when you enter a line beginning with Sub, the End Sub line is automatically inserted below.

4. This sets up a macro called **Box**. Click on the **View Microsoft Excel** icon to go back to Excel.

5. Check the macro works using **Tools, Macro, Macros.** Click on **Box, Run.**

6. Test that the UserForm works for all four buttons.

7. Go back to the Visual Basic Editor. Load the UserForm by double clicking on UserForm1 in the Project Explorer window.

8. Extend your UserForm and add an extra button. Edit the text on the button to read **Cancel**. Double click on the button and make the text as follows:

```
Private Sub CommandButton5_Click()
End
End Sub
```

> **Tip**
> ■ Set up an icon on the toolbars to run the **Box** macro. This will save time.

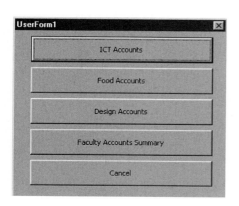

9. Save your file.

Each item on a UserForm such as a command button, a combo box or a text box is an object.

Each object has a unique name such as CommandButton1, TextBox6 or ComboBox4.

If you double click on the UserForm, you will
see the code for each object. It will appear as follows:

```
Private Sub CommandButton1_Click()
ICT
UserForm1.Hide
End Sub

Private Sub CommandButton2_Click()
Design
UserForm1.Hide
End Sub

Private Sub CommandButton3_Click()
Food
UserForm1.Hide
End Sub

Private Sub CommandButton4_Click()
Summary
UserForm1.Hide
End Sub

Private Sub CommandButton5_Click()
End
End Sub
```

Customising your UserForm

You can improve your UserForm in a number of ways for example by

➤ editing background colours;

➤ adding a caption instead of UserForm1;

➤ adding a label;

➤ changing the font;

➤ adding an image;

➤ resizing the UserForm.

The properties of each object are set up in the Properties Window.

> **WORKED EXAMPLE 2: Customising your UserForm**

1. Go back to the **Visual Basic Editor** and load the UserForm by double clicking on UserForm1 in the Project Explorer window.

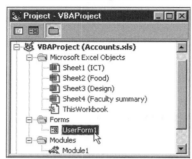

2. To edit the background colour, click on the UserForm. In the Properties Window (bottom left of screen), click on **BackColor**. Click on the drop-down arrow and choose Palette. You have a lot of colours to choose from.

3. Click on the drop down arrow at the top of the Properties Window where it says UserForm1 UserForm. Select a command button. Use the same method to change the colour of the button. Repeat this for the other buttons.

4. To edit the caption, click on the row called **Caption** in the Properties window and enter your text.

5. To add text, click on the Label icon in the Toolbox. Drag out a rectangle on the UserForm. Delete the word Label1 and enter your text. Go to the Properties window and edit the Font and the ForeColor. Use TextAlign in the Properties Window if you want to centre text.

6. Change the font of text on the command buttons in the same way.

7. To add a picture, click on the Image icon in the Toolbox, drag out a rectangle on the UserForm. Click on the row called **Picture** in the Properties window. Double click on the icon with three dots to select a picture. Find the picture you require. Choose **PictureSizeMode** 3 so that the picture resizes to fit.

8. Add a control tip text to your buttons using the Control Tip Text row of the Properties Window. Whatever you type in here appears on the screen as help text when you move the mouse over a control like a text box.

9. Resize the UserForm and the command buttons by dragging in the normal way.

10. Save your file.

UserForms can be made to look eye-catching as shown below.

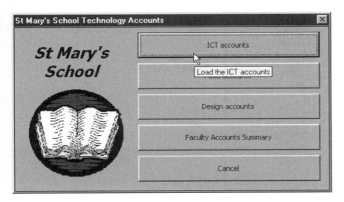

Using UserForms to enter data

In this section you will learn about how UserForms can be used to enter data into an Excel workbook.

Text boxes on a UserForm can be linked to cells in a spreadsheet and can be used for entering data.

Obviously you can just type the data straight into the cells, but using a UserForm can make it easier for the user and prevents data being entered into the wrong cells.

You can include other controls in a UserForm such as combo boxes and option buttons.

> ## WORKED EXAMPLE: The electronic markbook

	A	B	C	D
1	Surname	Forename	Form	Set
2	Brooks	Gemma	12A	2
3	Lee	Simon	12C	1
4	Overton	Christina	12A	3
5	Pinkett	Anita	12B	2
6	Rogers	Jennifer	12C	3
7	Tallent	Nathan	12A	1

	A	B
1	Sets	Forms
2	1	12A
3	2	12B
4	3	12C
5		12D

An electronic markbook will be used to store the names of students and their marks.

1. Enter the above data into Sheet1 of a new worksheet and name the cells from A2 to D7 as **Names**.

We need to set up the system to enter more students' names, which will automatically extend the named area downwards as more students are entered and sort the names into alphabetical order.

2. Enter the names of the forms and the sets into Sheet2 as shown. This data will be used later in setting up combo boxes.

3. Switch back to Sheet1 and save the file as **Classlist.xls**.

4. Load the **Visual Basic Editor** by pressing **ALT + F11**.

5. Choose **Insert, UserForm.** This will be called UserForm1.

6. Use the Properties Window to set the caption to Electronic markbook.

7. Add a picture and a title as in the previous unit.

8. Click on the **Text Box** icon in the Toolbar. Drag out a box at the top right of the UserForm as shown below.

9. With the box selected, set the Control Source in the **Properties Window** to **Sheet1!A3**.

10. Click on the Label icon and drag out a box above the text box. Enter the text **Surname** into the Label and change the font and colour as needed.

11. Add extra text boxes and labels as shown in the diagram below. The control source for **Forename** is Sheet1!B3 . The control source for **Form** is Sheet1!C3 . The control source for **Set** is Sheet1!D3 .

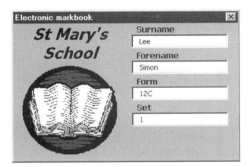

12. Adjust the size of the last two text boxes to suit the data.

13. Add a command button at the bottom of the UserForm. Double-click on this button and edit the code so that it is as follows:

```
Private Sub CommandButton1_Click()
UserForm1.Hide
Unload UserForm1
End Sub
```

14. Change the text on this button to **OK**.

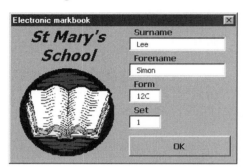

15. Save the UserForm.

16. Click on **Insert, Module**. Enter this macro:

```
Sub Details()
Load UserForm1
UserForm1.Show
End Sub
```

This sets up a macro called **Details** to enter the student details.

Save your file.

17. Click on the View Microsoft Excel icon to switch back into Excel and run the **Details** macro, by clicking on **Tools, Macro, Macros...** Check that it loads the new UserForm.

18. Close the UserForm by clicking on **OK**.

Setting up a macro to enter the names

We can now record a macro in Excel to enter new data. Remember it is always a good idea to work through the steps of the macro before you record it.

What will the macro do?

The macro will insert a blank row in the spreadsheet. It will load the UserForm. The user will enter the details and click on OK. The named area will be selected and sorted into alphabetical order by surname.

1. Click on **Tools, Macro, Record New Macro** and call the macro **AddNames.** Click on **OK**.

2. Select row 3 by clicking on the 3 in the row headings.

3. Click on **Insert, Rows**.

4. Run the **Details** macro using **Tools, Macro, Macros...** to load **UserForm1**.

5. Enter this data

Surname	Forename	Form	Set
Pemberton	Charles	12C	2

6. Click on **OK**.

7. Click on the drop down arrow in the **Name Box** and click on **Names**.

8. Click on **Data, Sort**. Make sure the **No header row** option is checked. Sort by **Surname** in ascending order.

9. Click off the data and stop recording the macro.

10. Add a button to run the **AddNames** macro.

11. Run the macro and add another name to the file to test it works.

Adding combo boxes to speed up data entry

As the set can only be 1, 2 or 3, we can replace the Set text box with a combo box (drop down box) giving a choice of 1, 2 or 3. This will speed up data entry and avoid mistakes. Set it up as follows:

1. With the **Classlist.xls** still loaded, load the **Visual Basic Editor**.

2. Double click on **UserForm1** in the Project Explorer window. If UserForm1 is not visible click on the + sign next to Forms.

3. Click on the **Set** text box. Press **Delete** on the keyboard.

4. Click on the Combo Box icon in the Toolbox.

5. Drag out a box on the UserForm to replace the deleted text box.

6. With the Combo box still selected, set the Control Source in the properties window to cell Sheet1!D3 and the Row Source to Sheet2!A2:A4

7. Test the UserForm to ensure that it works and the items in the drop down list are correct.

8. Improve the UserForm further by adding a drop down box for the form.

Running a system from a UserForm

In this section you will learn how to run a system from a UserForm.

WORKED EXAMPLE: The ideal weight problem

Problem statement

Fitness, diet and healthy eating magazines often produce tables of ideal weights according to a person's sex and height as shown below.

	A	B	C	D	E
1		Men		Women	
2		Min	Max	Min	Max
3	Height (cm)	Weight (kg)			
4	158	51	64	46	59
5	160	52	65	48	61
6	162	53	66	49	62
7	164	54	67	50	64
8	166	55	69	51	65
9	168	56	71	52	66
10	170	58	73	53	67
11	172	59	74	55	69
12	174	60	75	56	70
13	176	62	77	58	72
14	178	64	79	59	74
15	180	65	80	60	76
16	182	66	82	62	78
17	184	67	84	63	80

A system will be produced to allow a user to enter their sex and height.

The system will calculate from tables the user's ideal maximum and minimum weight range.

The output will be to screen with an option to print.

Brief design overview

A spinner will be used to enter a person's height in centimetres. It will be linked to cell J1.

Option buttons will be used to enter the user's Sex. This will be linked to cell J2 which will store TRUE if male and FALSE if female.

J3 will be used to decide which columns to lookup based on whether the user is male or female. The minimum weight for a man is in column 2. The minimum weight for a woman is in column 4. So if the user is a man, this cell will read 2. If the user is a woman, the cell will display 4.

Cell J4 will be used to lookup the minimum value from either column 2 or column 4.

Cell J5 will be used to lookup the maximum value from either column 3 or column 5.

Setting up the worksheet

1. Enter the details as shown above and save the file as **weight.xls**

2. Highlight the cells from A4 to E17 and give them the name **Table** using **Insert, Name, Define**

3. Enter 170 into J1.
   (This is the person's height.)

4. In J2 enter `TRUE`
   (TRUE represents Male, FALSE represents Female.)

5. In J3 enter `=IF(J2=TRUE,2,4)`
   (This shows which column to look in for the minimum weight. Column 2 for male, column 4 for female.)

6. In J4 enter `=VLOOKUP(J1,table,J3)`
   (This looks up the minimum weight in either column 2 or column 4.)

7. In J5 enter `=VLOOKUP(J1,table,J3+1)`
   (This looks up the maximum weight in either column 3 or column 5.)

The formulas are shown below:

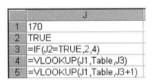

	J
1	170
2	TRUE
3	=IF(J2=TRUE,2,4)
4	=VLOOKUP(J1,Table,J3)
5	=VLOOKUP(J1,Table,J3+1)

The lookups in J4 and J5 look up the minimum and maximum weights for the height in J1. For a height of 170, they should read 58 and 73 if male.

Setting up the UserForm

1. Load the Visual Basic Editor Window by clicking on **Tools, Macro, Visual Basic Editor** or pressing ALT + F11

2. Click on **Insert, UserForm** or click on the **Insert UserForm** icon.

3. In the properties window, set the Caption to **Your Ideal Weight**.

4. Use a Label to put the title **What is your ideal weight?** at the top of your UserForm.

5. In the properties window, set the font size for the label to 16.
   The UserForm will look like this:

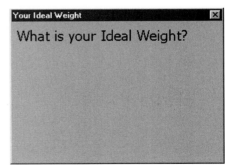

Setting up the spinner to adjust the height

1. Click on the Spin Button icon on the Toolbox and drag out a Spinner near the top of the UserForm. If the spinner is pointing horizontally, hold down the ALT key and resize the spinner so that it points vertically.

2. With the spinner still selected, set Max in the properties window to `184`, Min to `158`, Small Change to `2` and then set the Control Source to `J1`.

3. Double click on the spinner and edit the text to read as follows:

```
Private Sub SpinButton_Change()
Range("J1").Value = SpinButton1.Value
End Sub
```

This means that as you click the spinner, the value in cell J1 updates immediately.

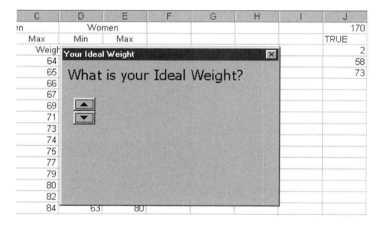

4. Click on the **Close** icon to return to the UserForm

5. Click on the **Run Sub/UserForm** icon to load the UserForm and test the spinner. It should alter the numbers in J1, J4 and J5.

6. Close the UserForm by clicking on the close icon. Save your file by clicking on the save icon.

7. Click on the Text Box icon in the Toolbox and drag out a small Text Box underneath the spinner as shown below and set the Control Source in the properties window to J1

8. Add a label to your spinner as shown left.

9. Click on the Run Sub/UserForm icon to test that the number in the text box goes up or down by 2 when the spinner is clicked. Save your file.

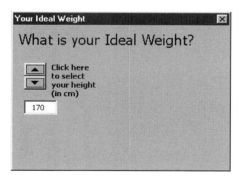

Adding option buttons for male and female

1. Click on the Option Button icon in the Toolbox and add an option button to your UserForm. Edit the label to **Male** Set the Control Source to **J2**

2. Add another option button labelled **Female** You must not set the Control Source. Click on the **Run Sub/UserForm** icon to test that as you choose Female, the numbers change in J4 and J5. Save your file.

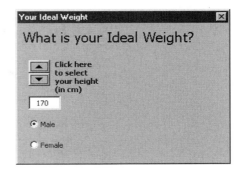

Adding list boxes for the LOOKUPS

1. Click on the List Box icon in the Toolbox and add a **list box** to your UserForm as shown. Set the **Row Source** set to **J4**.

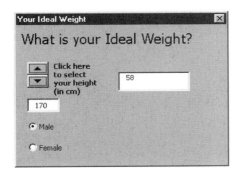

2. Add another list box with Row Source J5 and add labels as shown.

3. Click on the Run Sub/UserForm icon to test that as you click on the spinner, the maximum and minimum weights change. Save your file.

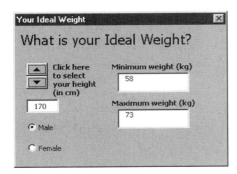

Note: When linking a UserForm box to a cell with a formula or a lookup, use a **list box**.

Adding Command Buttons

1. Click on the Command Button icon in the Toolbox to add a command button. Edit the text on the button to **Print**.

2. Double click on buttton. Edit the text so that it reads as follows:

```
Private Sub CommandButton1_Click()
UserForm1.PrintForm
End Sub
```

3. Add another command button. Edit the text on the button to Exit

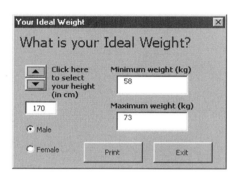

4. Double click on button. Edit the text so that it reads as follows:

```
Private Sub CommandButton2_Click()
Application.Quit
End Sub
```

5. Save your file. Click on the Run Sub/UserForm icon and test the buttons.

Finishing the system

1. Click on the Image icon in the Toolbox to add an image to your UserForm. Use the picture property to select the image.

2. Enlarge the fonts of list boxes and centre the text as shown.

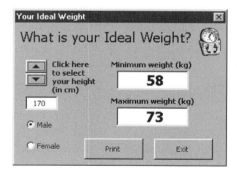

3. Click on **Insert, Module** This opens a Visual Basic Editor window where macro coding is entered and stored.

4. Enter this macro in the Visual Basic Editor window:

```
Sub Auto_open()
Load UserForm1
UserForm1.Show
End Sub
```

5. Go back to Excel by clicking on the **View Microsoft Excel** icon.

6. Remove the gridlines by clicking on **Tools, Options** and unchecking **Gridlines**

7. Highlight all the cells and set the text colour to white.

8. Save your file.

9. Close the file. Reload the file and test that the system works.

Ideas for further development

You can develop the system further by:

- Removing row and column headings

- Removing the toolbars

- Removing the scrollbars

- Removing the status bar, formula bar and tabs

- Adding a second sheet storing the heights and weights in Imperial units

- Setting up a UserForm for the user to select either Imperial or metric units

Scenarios and pivot tables

In this chapter you will learn how to use scenarios to save different versions of the same worksheet.

▶ WORKED EXAMPLE: Setting up scenarios

	A	B	C	D	E
1			Hotel Manhattan		
2	Type of room	Price per night	No of rooms	Income if full	
3	Single room	67	42	=C3*B3	
4	Double room	87	31	=C4*B4	
5	Suite	120	3	=C5*B5	
6	Penthouse	250	1	=C6*B6	
7				=SUM(D3:D6)	
8					
9	Season	Month	No of days	Forecast occupancy	Revenue
10	High season	May to September	153	1	=D10*C10*D7
11	Low season	October to April	212	1	=D11*C11*D7
12					=SUM(E10:E11)

The Hotel Manhattan wants to plan their cash-flow. Their occupancy rates are around 70 to 80 per cent in summer and 50 to 60 per cent in winter. They can store various predictions for their income using **Scenarios.**

1. Set up the spreadsheet as shown above.

2. Format cells B3 to B6, D3 to D7 and E10 to E12 as currency.

3. Format cells D10 to D11 as percentages. (They will say 100%).

The hotel has decided to save predictions based on:

◀ 70 per cent occupancy all year round;

◀ 60 per cent occupancy all year round;

◀ 50 per cent occupancy all year round;

◀ 70 per cent occupancy in high season and 50 per cent occupancy in low season.

We can set up four different **scenarios** to help them. To set up scenarios:

1. Click on **Tools, Scenarios.** You will see this box

2. No scenarios exist at present so we need to add some. Click on **Add...**

3. Enter the name of the scenario – **70 per cent occupancy** – and the names of the two changing cells into the dialogue box.

4. Click on **OK**.

5. Enter the values for each of the changing cells and click on **OK**.

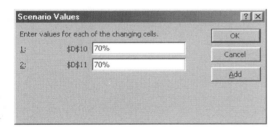

6. Add three more scenarios with the appropriate data.

7. If you click on **Summary...** you will set up a new worksheet with a summary of all the scenarios. First this screen appears:

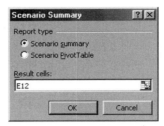

8. E12 is the cell with the total amount of the bill stored in it. This is the figure we want in our summary but we could click on any cell. Click on **OK**.

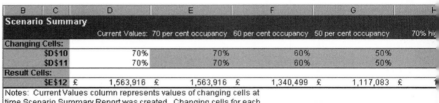

B	C	D	E	F	G	H
Scenario Summary						
		Current Values:	70 per cent occupancy	60 per cent occupancy	50 per cent occupancy	70% hi
Changing Cells:						
	D10	70%	70%	60%	50%	
	D11	70%	70%	60%	50%	
Result Cells:						
	E12 £	1,563,916 £	1,563,916 £	1,340,499 £	1,117,083 £	

Notes: Current Values column represents values of changing cells at time Scenario Summary Report was created. Changing cells for each scenario are highlighted in gray.

The summary looks like this:
To load any of the scenarios:

1. Go back to sheet 1.

2. Click on **Tools, Scenarios**.

3. Click on the scenario required.

4. Click on **Show**.

5. Click on **Close**.

> **Note**
>
> ■ The scenario summary does not update as you change figures in the invoice. You will need to click on **Tools**, **Scenario** again and click on **Summary...** This will set up a new worksheet called Scenario Summary 2.

Exercise 16.1

Scenarios exercise:

1. Load the file from Unit 1 called vending.xls

	A	B	C	D	E	F	G	H	I	J	K
1		Mon	Tue	Wed	Thu	Fri	Total sales	Cost price	Sell price	Profit per can	Total profit
2	Cola	10	10	10	10	10	50	£0.17	£ 0.50	£ 0.33	£ 16.50
3	Diet Cola	10	10	10	10	10	50	£0.16	£ 0.50	£ 0.34	£ 17.00
4	Sunkist	10	10	10	10	10	50	£0.18	£ 0.50	£ 0.32	£ 16.00
5	Lilt	10	10	10	10	10	50	£0.18	£ 0.50	£ 0.32	£ 16.00
6	Cherry Cola	10	10	10	10	10	50	£0.15	£ 0.50	£ 0.35	£ 17.50
7						Total cans sold	250			Weekly profit	£ 83.00

2. Save scenarios based on prices of:

- 30p per can
- 40p per can
- 50p per can
- 60p per can

3. Produce a Scenario Summary of the weekly profit.

Pivot tables

In this section you will learn how to use pivot tables to group large amounts of data in an easy to read table. For example, the Hotel Manhattan has this file of its employees:

	A	B	C	D	E	F	G	H
1	EMPL NO	SURNAME	FORENAME	DEPT	SALARY	DOB	POST	M/F
2	000262	Bird	Linda	Restaurant	13600	17/02/76	Chef	F
3	000159	Caulder	Fraser	Restaurant	14200	05/06/41	Chef	M
4	000267	Clark	Sarah	Reception	11090	31/10/42	Receptionist	F
5	000297	Cook	Sally	Accommodation	9200	17/06/53	Cleaner	F
6	000141	Dyson	Angela	Restaurant	8200	19/02/58	Waitress	F
7	000011	Green	Julie	Accommodation	9200	20/06/61	Cleaner	F
8	000185	Johnson	Rebecca	Restaurant	7900	22/12/49	Waitress	F
9	000118	Jones	Robert	Restaurant	7400	17/08/69	Waiter	M
10	000367	Khan	Wahir	Restaurant	12200	31/12/58	Chef	M
11	000034	Noble	Marie	Restaurant	8150	14/06/62	Waitress	F
12	000281	Patel	Niru	Restaurant	7600	01/05/78	Waitress	F
13	000245	Powell	Sharon	Reception	12000	11/01/66	Receptionist	F
14	000444	Robertson	Richard	Reception	14125	18/07/60	Security Officer	M
15	000555	Robinson	Damion	Reception	11075	14/04/78	Doorman	M
16	000190	Sands	Elizabeth	Accommodation	8500	04/04/67	Cleaner	F
17	000247	Sands	Elaine	Accommodation	9600	18/12/62	Cleaner	F

A pivot table will allow us to group this information by department, by post and by sex to analyse exactly where the hotel pays wages.

1. Enter the data and save it as **workers.xls**.

2. Highlight the data and click on **Data, Pivot Table and Pivot Chart Report. (Data, Pivot Table Report** in Excel 97.).

3. It loads a wizard. Select **Microsoft Excel list or database** if not already selected and click on **Next**.

4. The next stage of the wizard ask where is the data that you want to use. Click on **Next**.

Hints

- To enter 000262, type in an apostrophe first – '000262.

- If the date of birth appears as 17-Feb, highlight column F and click on **Format, Cells, Date** and choose the correct format.

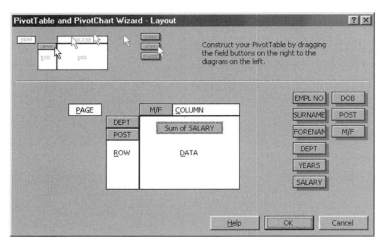

5. In Excel 97 this table appears. In Excel 2000 click on **New worksheet** and click on **Layout.** The table loads.

6. This is where you choose which data to group and display. Drag the fieldnames, **Dept** and **Post** to where it says ROW, as in the diagram below. Drag **M/F** to where it says COLUMN and drag **Salary** to where it says DATA. When you drag **Salary** onto the middle of the page it becomes **Sum of Salary**.

7. Click on **OK** and then click on **Finish.**

The pivot table will look like this:

3	Sum of SALARY		M/F		
4	DEPT	POST	F	M	Grand Total
5	Accommodation	Cleaner	36500		36500
6	Accommodation Total		36500		36500
7	Reception	Doorman		11075	11075
8		Receptionist	23090		23090
9		Security Officer		14125	14125
10	Reception Total		23090	25200	48290
11	Restaurant	Chef	13600	26400	40000
12		Waiter		7400	7400
13		Waitress	31850		31850
14	Restaurant Total		45450	33800	79250
15	Grand Total		105040	59000	164040

At a glance we can see total salaries paid, by department, by post and by sex.

 Pivot table exercise

Exercise 16.2

1. The different departments of a company are charged on the basis of hours of internet use. The company has to distinguish between use for e-mail and use for the world-wide web. Using the data in this table, set up a pivot table to group the data, to show Internet, intranet and total use for each department split into www and e-mail.

	A	B	C	D	E	F	G
1	**Forename**	**Surname**	**Section**	**Type**	**Intranet Use**	**Internet Use**	**Total**
2	Angela	Jones	Admin	e-mail	4	6	
3	Bertie	Galley	Finance	www	23	2	
4	Heather	Jones	Security	e-mail	2	7	
5	Bill	Brown	Sales	e-mail	3	3	
6	Eileen	Sands	Sales	e-mail	16	4	
7	Elizabeth	Bird	Finance	e-mail	3	1	
8	Charles	Bryant	Marketing	www	32	2	
9	Maria	Chambers	Finance	e-mail	21	9	
10	Darren	Foreman	Finance	www	17	2	
11	Olive	Hassent	Sales	e-mail	8	0	
12	Katie	Johnson	Marketing	e-mail	10	3	
13	Quinton	Harris	Sales	www	8	7	

Using Excel as a database

In this section you will cover:

✔ setting up, sorting and searching a database;

✔ using Data Forms;

✔ using AutoFilter;

✔ using the Advanced Filter;

✔ database Functions.

A spreadsheet lends itself to storing and sorting lists of information, such as employees, customers, cars, students and so on.

More commonly files or lists such as this are called databases, Excel calls them **lists**.

▶ Creating a data list

We are going to set up a simple **file** of properties for sale.

Each **record** in the file or row in the spreadsheet will hold details of the property.

The **fields** or columns in the spreadsheet will be Estate Agent, Area, Type, No of Bedrooms, Price

	A	B	C	D	E
1	Agent	Area	Type	Bedrooms	Price
2	Hall & Partners	Mickleover	detached	3	170000
3	Bradford & Bingley	Oakwood	detached	4	92950
4	Ashley Adams	Mickleover	bungalow	3	86950
5	Halifax	Littleover	semi-detached	3	60000
6	Hall & Partners	Mickleover	semi-detached	2	52950

Note

■ When you enter the data you will notice that Excel stores previously entered data and carries out an AutoComplete for you. This saves you having to type in all the data. This can be turned off/on by choosing **Tools, Options**, clicking the **Edit tab** and checking the enable **AutoComplete**.

■ Calculated fields can be added by setting up the formulas in the appropriate column

Sorting the file

Sorting can be done on the whole file or a named range of cells.

To produce a sorted list of houses by price:

1. Load or set up the file **houses.xls**
   (see page 107).

2. Click in cell A1 and click on **Data, Sort**

3. Click on the down arrow on the Sort by box, choose **Price** and
   click on **Descending**, click **OK**.

It is also possible to sort on more than one field.

1. Load the file **houses.xls** or **Edit, Undo** the previous sort.

2. From the menu choose **Data, Sort**.

3. Click on the down arrow on the Sort by box, choose **Agent** and
   click on **Ascending**.

4. Click on the down arrow on the next Sort by box, choose **Price**
   and click on **Descending** and click **OK**.

This should produce a list sorted by Agent and then by price as below.

	A	B	C	D	E
1	**Agent**	**Area**	**Type**	**Bedrooms**	**Price**
2	Ashley Adams	Mickleover	bungalow	3	86950
3	Ashley Adams	Mickleover	bungalow	3	86950
4	Ashley Adams	Allestree	semi-detached	3	82500
5	Ashley Adams	Etwall	semi-detached	3	65000
6	Ashley Adams	Mickleover	semi-detached	3	59950
7	Bagshaws	Etwall	detached	4	197500
8	Bagshaws	Etwall	detached	4	189950

Using a Data Form to search and edit a file.

1. Load the file **houses.xls**.

2. From the menu choose **Data, Form**.

Click on **Find Next** to take you to details of the next house

Click on **Find Prev** to take you to details of the previous house

Click on **Delete** to enable you to remove a house from file

Click on **New** to allow you to enter details of a new property (Press Tab between entering fields).

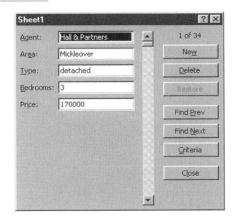

You can use the Data Form to do simple searches

1. Click on criteria and a blank form loads.

2. Enter **Etwall** in the field area and click on **Find Next** to scroll through the houses in Etwall.

You can narrow down the search.

3. Click on criteria again and enter 3 in the **Bedrooms** field.

4. You can now scroll through the three bedroom houses in Etwall.

Database Exercise 1

Exercise 17.1

Use the Data Form to answer the following:

1. Produce details of all houses for sale in Oakwood. How many are there?

2. A customer wants details of detached houses for sale in Mickleover. How many are there and what price are they?

3. A customer wants to purchase a house with 3 bedrooms in Littleover, search for details. How many are there and what price are they?

Using AutoFilter to search the database

1. Load the file **houses.xls**.

2. Click on **Data, Filter, AutoFilter**

    Drop down boxes appear by each field name. If you click the arrow it will give you a list of items in that field.

	A	B	C	D	E
1	Agent	Area	Type	Bedroom	Price
2	Ashley Adams	Mickleover	bungalow	3	86950
3	Ashley Adams	Mickleover	bungalow	3	86950
4	Ashley Adams	Allestree	semi-detached	3	82500
5	Ashley Adams	Etwall	semi-detached	3	65000
6	Ashley Adams	Mickleover	semi-detached	3	59950

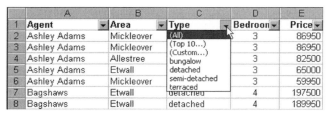

It is easy to build up quick searches e.g. bungalows in Mickleover.

1. Click on the Area field drop down and choose **Mickleover**.

2. Then click on the Type field drop down and choose **bungalow**.

You should get the results on the left.

Excel hides the rows that do not meet the criteria and displays the row numbers in blue.

To restore your data click on **Data, Filter, Show All**.

It is possible to do more advanced searching by choosing the custom option.

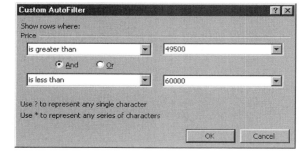

■ FILTER 1

Suppose we wish to find properties in Mickleover or Littleover.

1. Choose the **Area** drop down and click on **Custom**.

2. The dialog box below appears, fill in as shown.

The search produces 18 houses

■ FILTER 2

Suppose we wish to find properties with the price between £49500 and £60000

1. Restore your data.

2. Click on the **Price** drop down and click on **Custom**.

3. The dialog box below appears. Fill it in as shown on the left.

Five houses should be found.

▪ Some hints on using AutoFilter.

If you only wish to use one column for filtering you can remove the other column drop downs. Click on the column heading you wish to search on. Then choose **Data, Filter, AutoFilter**.

To remove AutoFilter for a particular column, click on (**All**) from the drop down list.

To remove all AutoFilters, click on **Data**, **Filter, Show All**.

You can use **AutoFilter** to find blank fields. If a column contains blanks you will see the entries (Blanks) and (NonBlanks) in the columns drop down list.

If you wish to remove rows with blank entries then choose **NonBlanks**.

If you wish to find rows in which a column has a no entry then choose **Blanks**.

Autofiltered data can be copied and pasted to other areas of the worksheet in the usual way. To automate this process you need to use the **Advanced Filter** option.

 Database Exercise 2

Use **AutoFilter** and the file **houses.xls** to answer the following:

1. A customer wants details of houses for sale in Etwall. How many are there?

2. A customer wants to purchase a house with four bedrooms. Search for details. How many are there?

3. A customer requires details of detached houses in Mickleover. Search for details.

4. A customer requires a three bedroomed house in Littleover. Search for details.

Exercise 17.2

▪ The advanced filter option

The advanced filter command allows you to search on more than two fields and offers increased options. The command can also be used to automate the moving of filtered data to another part of the worksheet.

▶ A WORKED EXAMPLE

The first step is to define the cells that make up the database. This is called the **list range**.

1. Using the file **houses.xls** highlight the cells A1 to E35.

2. From the **Insert** menu choose **Name, Define** and call the range **Database** and click **OK**.

The next stage is to set up and define the **criteria range** this is the range of cells which will store your search conditions.

Select the row headings in row 1 and copy and paste them to an area below your data list. We have chosen row 39.

In the rows below enter the search conditions as shown. This will produce a list of bungalows in Littleover.

	Agent	Area	Type	Bedrooms	Price
35	Ashley Adams	Mickleover	semi-detached	3	59950
36					
37					
38					
39	**Agent**	**Area**	**Type**	**Bedrooms**	**Price**
40		Littleover	bungalow		
41					

Name the range A39 to E40 **criteria**.

Click on **Data, Filter, Advanced Filter**.

Enter the ranges shown.

Clicking on **OK** should produce the filtered list below which displays one property. The selected row is highlighted in blue.

	Agent	Area	Type	Bedrooms	Price
1	**Agent**	**Area**	**Type**	**Bedrooms**	**Price**
3	Raybould & Sons	Littleover	bungalow	3	132000
36					
37					
38					
39	**Agent**	**Area**	**Type**	**Bedrooms**	**Price**
40		Littleover	bungalow		

Searches can be built up in the same way.

The search criteria below will list three bedroomed properties in Littleover or Mickleover.

	Agent	Area	Type	Bedrooms	Price
38					
39	Agent	Area	Type	Bedrooms	Price
40		Mickleover		3	
41		Etwall		3	
42					

The criteria range is now A39: E41.

▶ Database Exercise 3

Exercise 17.3

Use the advanced filter option to answer the following questions:

1. A customer requires a three bedroomed house in Littleover or Mickleover. Search for details.

2. A customer requires a property in the Allestree, Darley Abbey area. Search for details.

3. A customer requires a three bedroomed detached property in Mickleover. Search for details.

▶ Copying data to another location

1. Set up the search as shown below to find three bedroom properties in Etwall or Mickleover.

	Agent	Area	Type	Bedrooms	Price
38					
39	Agent	Area	Type	Bedrooms	Price
40		Mickleover		3	
41		Etwall		3	
42					

2. Make sure your named criteria range is A39 to E41.

3. From the Data menu choose **Filter, Advanced Filter**.

4. In the dialog box check **Copy to another location** and enter **A44** in the **Copy to** box.

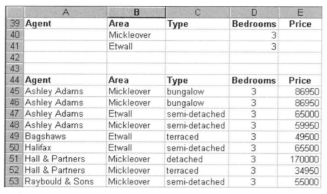

The search should produce these results:

The output from the search is displayed in row 44 which now becomes the named area **Extract**. Check by clicking the name box drop down.

	A	B	C	D	E
39	Agent	Area	Type	Bedrooms	Price
40		Mickleover		3	
41		Etwall		3	
42					
43					
44	Agent	Area	Type	Bedrooms	Price
45	Ashley Adams	Mickleover	bungalow	3	86950
46	Ashley Adams	Mickleover	bungalow	3	86950
47	Ashley Adams	Etwall	semi-detached	3	65000
48	Ashley Adams	Mickleover	semi-detached	3	59950
49	Bagshaws	Etwall	terraced	3	49500
50	Halifax	Etwall	semi-detached	3	65500
51	Hall & Partners	Mickleover	detached	3	170000
52	Hall & Partners	Mickleover	terraced	3	34950
53	Raybould & Sons	Mickleover	semi-detached	3	55000

It is now possible to vary the criteria in the criteria range. Try changing the criteria to produce the output shown on the left.

	A	B	C	D	E
39	Agent	Area	Type	Bedrooms	Price
40		Mickleover		2	
41		Etwall		2	
42					
43					
44	Agent	Area	Type	Bedrooms	Price
45	Bagshaws	Etwall	terraced	2	45000
46	Halifax	Etwall	semi-detached	2	55500
47	Halifax	Mickleover	terraced	2	33950
48	Hall & Partners	Mickleover	semi-detached	2	52950

■ Using the database functions

Excel provides a number of **d** or **database** functions. Examples are **DCOUNT**, **DAVERAGE**, **DSUM**, **DMAX**, **DMIN**.

Database functions take the form `=Function(database,"field",criteria)` where:

◢ **Database** is the name of database range you have defined;

◢ **Field** is the column you wish to operate on;

◢ **Criteria** is the criteria range you have defined.

Worked example

We are going to use the database functions to analyse house prices in the Mickleover area.

1. Set up the criteria and headings as shown below.

	Agent	Area	Type	Bedrooms	Price
39	Agent	Area	Type	Bedrooms	Price
40		Mickleover		3	
41					
42					
43	Number of houses				
44	Average price				
45	Maximum price				
46	Minimum price				
47	Total value				

2. Make sure you have named the **database** and **criteria** ranges (A1:E45 and A39:E40).

3. Select cell **B43**.

4. From the **Insert** menu choose **Function**.

The paste Function box appears right.

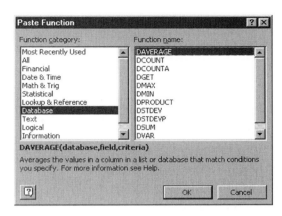

5. Click on **Database** in the left hand list and click on **DCOUNT** from the Function names and enter the details as below.

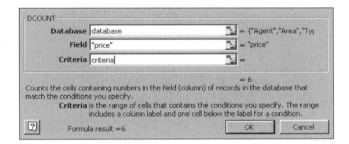

The formula will appear in the formula bar as
`=DCOUNT(database,"price",Criteria)`

In the same way use the function **DAVERAGE** to return the average house price in cell D44.

Use the functions **DMAX** and **DMIN** to return maximum and minimum house prices in cells D45 and D46.

In cell D47, use **DSUM** to total the house values.

The results should appear as below:

39	Agent	Area	Type	Bedrooms	Price
40		Mickleover		3	
41					
42					
43	Number of houses	6			
44	Average price	82300			
45	Maximum price	170000			
46	Minimum price	34950			
47	Total value	493800			

When it works, try varying the search criteria, e.g. change the area to Littleover or the number of bedrooms to two.

The houses.xls file

Agent	Area	Type	Bedrooms	Price
Raybould & Sons	Hulland Ward	semi-detached	5	245000
Bagshaws	Etwall	detached	4	197500
Bagshaws	Etwall	detached	4	189950
Hall & Partners	Mickleover	detached	3	170000
Raybould & Sons	Littleover	bungalow	3	132000
Raybould & Sons	Etwall	detached	4	127000
Raybould & Sons	Willington	semi-detached	3	117500
Bradford & Bingley	Littleover	detached	5	99950
Bradford & Bingley	Oakwood	detached	4	92950
Bradford & Bingley	Oakwood	detached	4	92950
Ashley Adams	Mickleover	bungalow	3	86950
Ashley Adams	Mickleover	bungalow	3	86950
Bradford & Bingley	Borrowash	detached	3	85000
Ashley Adams	Allestree	semi-detached	3	82500
Bradford & Bingley	Mickleover	detached	5	79950
Bradford & Bingley	Littleover	detached	3	75950
Halifax	Etwall	semi-detached	3	65500
Ashley Adams	Etwall	semi-detached	3	65000
Halifax	Littleover	semi-detached	3	60000
Halifax	Littleover	semi-detached	3	60000
Halifax	Littleover	semi-detached	3	60000
Hall & Partners	Egginton	detached	3	59999
Ashley Adams	Mickleover	semi-detached	3	59950
Halifax	Etwall	semi-detached	2	55500
Raybould & Sons	Mickleover	semi-detached	3	55000
Hall & Partners	Mickleover	semi-detached	2	52950
Bagshaws	Etwall	terraced	3	49500
Hall & Partners	Littleover	terraced	2	48500
Halifax	Littleover	semi-detached	3	47500
Bagshaws	Darley Abbey	detached	4	46000
Bagshaws	Etwall	terraced	2	45000
Hall & Partners	Mickleover	terraced	3	34950
Halifax	Mickleover	terraced	2	33950
Hall & Partners	Littleover	terraced	2	32950

Setting up the car insurance quotation system

The student should remember that the system demonstrated here is not being put forward for a particular grade at any level. It is fictitious and aims to show how the software features in Excel can be incorporated to produce a working system.

The system is made up of the following tasks:

1. Setting up the Insurance Groups worksheet

2. Setting up the Multipliers worksheet

3. Setting up the Quotes worksheet

4. Preparing the quote – setting up the LOOKUP table

5. Preparing the quote – entering the multipliers

6. Calculating the total cost

7. Setting up the Customer worksheet

8. Automating the filing of quotes

9. Clearing the current screen to enter a new quote

10. Designing the printed quote

11. Adding user options to the quotes screen

12. Customising the interface and some finishing touches

13. Adding a front end

Note: throughout the system development students are advised to keep a test log and record details of any tests carried out.

1. Setting up the Insurance Groups worksheet

1. The user has provided data about the makes, models and insurance groups of cars. Enter the data into a worksheet as shown below. (Of course a real system would have far more cars.)

	A	B	C	D
1	Number	Make	Model	IG
2	1	Peugeot	106	3
3	2	Peugeot	206	3
4	3	Peugeot	306	4
5	4	Peugeot	406	10
6	5	Peugeot	806	10
7	6	Ford	Ka	2
8	7	Ford	Fiesta	4
9	8	Ford	Escort	5
10	9	Ford	Puma	9
11	10	Ford	Focus	5
12	11	Ford	Mondeo	8
13	12	Ford	Galaxy	11
14	13	Honda	Civic	9
15	14	Honda	Prelude	14
16	15	Honda	Accord	8
17	16	Reliant	Robin	6
18	17	Rover	100	3
19	18	Rover	200	6
20	19	Rover	400	8
21	20	Rover	800	12
22				

2. Rename the worksheet **Groups** by double clicking on the sheet tab.

We are going to use a simplified format of the concatenate function to combine the Make and Model columns to give the full car name in column E.

3. In cell E2 enter =B2&" "&C2 . Make sure there is a space between the apostrophes.

4. Copy the formula down the column by highlighting cells E2 to E21 and from the menu choosing **Edit, Fill, Down**.

5. The column will need widening, click **Format, Column, AutoFit Selection** and enter the heading **Car Name** in cell E1.

6. Highlight the cells A1 to E21 and define them using the name **Groups** by clicking **Insert, Name, Define.**

We now need to add the insurance group costs.

7. Enter the details as shown below in cells H1 to I21.

8. Highlight the cells H1 to I21 and define them using the name **Costs** by clicking **Insert, Name, Define**.

Your finished spreadsheet should look as below.

Number	Make	Model	IG	CarName			IG	Basic Cost
1	Peugeot	106	3	Peugeot 106			1	£ 174.00
2	Peugeot	206	3	Peugeot 206			2	£ 180.00
3	Peugeot	306	4	Peugeot 306			3	£ 187.00
4	Peugeot	406	10	Peugeot 406			4	£ 194.00
5	Peugeot	806	10	Peugeot 806			5	£ 202.00
6	Ford	Ka	2	Ford Ka			6	£ 210.00
7	Ford	Fiesta	4	Ford Fiesta			7	£ 222.00
8	Ford	Escort	5	Ford Escort			8	£ 235.00
9	Ford	Puma	9	Ford Puma			9	£ 248.00
10	Ford	Focus	5	Ford Focus			10	£ 264.00
11	Ford	Mondeo	8	Ford Mondeo			11	£ 280.00
12	Ford	Galaxy	11	Ford Galaxy			12	£ 3?? ??
13	Honda	Civic	9	Honda Civic			13	£ 324.00
14	Honda	Prelude	14	Honda Prelude			14	£ 362.00
15	Honda	Accord	8	Honda Accord			15	£ 417.00
16	Reliant	Robin	6	Reliant Robin			16	£ 493.00
17	Rover	100	3	Rover 100			17	£ 600.00
18	Rover	200	6	Rover 200			18	£ 720.00
19	Rover	400	8	Rover 400			19	£ 838.00
20	Rover	800	12	Rover 800			20	£ 945.00

`Groups / Sheet2 / Sheet3 /`

▶ 2. Setting up the Multipliers

1. Double click on the tab for Sheet2.

This sheet will store the multipliers used in calculating the insurance quote.

2. Rename the worksheet **Multipliers** by double clicking on the sheet tab.

3. Enter the data into cells A1 to D34 as shown on the right.

	A	B	C	D
1		Age	Multiplier	
2	1	17-19	4.8	
3	2	20-24	2.40	
4	3	25-29	2.00	
5	4	30-34	1.50	
6	5	35-39	1.30	
7	6	40-44	1.20	
8	7	45-49	1.15	
9	8	50-54	1.10	
10	9	55-59	1.05	
11	10	60-65	1.00	
12				
13				
14		Sex	Multiplier	
15	1	Male	1.30	
16	2	Female	1.00	
17				
18				
19		Area	Multiplier	
20	1	High risk	2.40	
21	2	Medium risk	1.70	
22	3	Low risk	1.00	
23				
24		No Claim Bonus	Multiplier	
25		0	0%	
26		1	30%	
27		2	40%	
28		3	50%	
29		4	60%	
30				
31		Type	Multiplier	Abbrev
32	1	Fully comprehensive	1	FC
33	2	Third party, fire & theft	0.46	TPFT
34	3	Third party only	0.39	TP

`Groups \ Multipliers / Sheet3 /`

3. Setting up the Quotes worksheet

	A	B	C	D
1				
2				
3				
4				
5				
6			Forename	
7			Surname	
8			Address 1	
9			Address 2	
10			Postcode	

The next stage is to design the sheet which will display and calculate the quote.

1. Click on the tab for Sheet3 and rename the worksheet **Quotes**.

2. Enter the data as shown left and set the width of column D to 20.

Adding the option buttons

Option boxes will be added to allow the user to select male or female.

1. In cell C12 enter the label Sex.

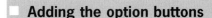

2. From the menu click **View, Toolbars, Forms** and select the **Option Button**.

	A	B	C	D	E
1					
2					
3					
4					
5					
6			Forename		
7			Surname		
8			Address 1		
9			Address 2		
10			Postcode		
11				⊙ Male	
12			Sex	○ Female	1

3. Drag out two option buttons over cells D11 and D12, label one Male and the other Female.

4. Right click on one option button to call up the short cut menu (shown bottom left), click on **Format Control** and set the cell link to E12.

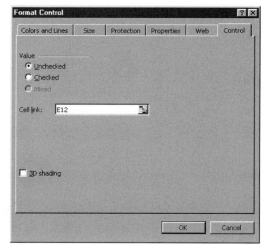

Adding combo boxes

Combo boxes are now added to allow the user to select the type of car and age group of the driver.

1. In cell C14 enter the label Car.

2. From the menu click on **View, Toolbars, Forms** and select **Combo Box**.

3. Drag out a combo box over cell D14.

4. Right click on the combo box to call up the short cut menu, click on **Format Control** and set the cell link to E14 and set the input range to Groups!E2:E21

5. In cell C16 enter the label Age.

6. Drag out another combo box over cell D16 and link the control to E16.

7. Enter the input range as Multipliers!B2:B11 . This can be done by switching to the sheet multipliers and dragging across the cell range B2 to B11.

Your sheet should appear as below.

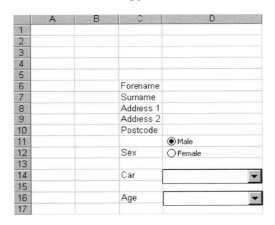

Adding list boxes

List boxes are now added to allow the user to select the area of risk and insurance types.

1. In cell C18 enter Area and in cell C20 enter Type.
2. From the menu choose **View, Toolbars, Form** and select **List Box**.

3. Drag out a list box over cell D18. Link the control to cell E18.Enter the input range as Multipliers!B20:B22
4. Drag out another list box over cells D20. Link the control to cell E20. Enter the input range as Multipliers!B32:B34
5. Use the handles on the controls to position and resize as necessary.

Adding a check box

A check box will be used to declare an extra driver.

1. In cell C22 enter the label Driver.
2. From the menu click **View, Toolbars, Forms** and select **Check Box**.

3. Drag out a check box over cell D22 and link the control to E22. Change the label to **Extra Driver.**

At this stage your spreadsheet should appear as below.

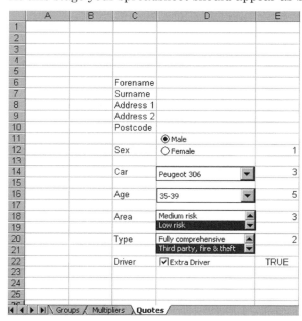

Adding a spinner

A spinner will be used to set the years no claims bonus where appropriate.

A **LOOKUP** function will find the percentage discount allowed depending on the years' no claims bonus.

1. In cell C24 enter the heading No Claims. In D23 and E23 enter the headings Years and Percent. Right align Years and centre Percent.

2. From the menu click **View, Toolbars, Forms** and select **Spinner**.

3. Drag out a spinner control over cell D24.

4. Link the spinner to cell D24. Set the maximum value to 4, minimum value to 0 and increment 1. This implies that a driver can have up to 4 years no claims bonus.

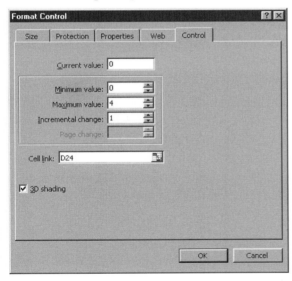

5. In cell E24 enter the formula =VLOOKUP(D24,Multipliers!B25:C29,2) and format the cell to percentage.

This function will look in the multipliers sheet for the percentage discount available.

NB The sheet at present may look a little untidy and cramped, we will deal with the layout later.

▶ 4. Preparing the quote – setting up the LOOKUP table

	F
6	Make
7	Model
8	IG
9	Sex
10	Age
11	Risk
12	Extra Driver
13	No claims
14	Type

1. In cells F6 to F14 enter the factors shown on the left needed to calculate the insurance quotes.

2. In G6 enter the formula: `=VLOOKUP(E14,groups,2)`

This will pick up the numeric value of the car chosen which is stored in E14, find it in the named area groups and return the make from the second column.

3. In G7 enter the formula: `=VLOOKUP(E14,groups,3)`

This will pick up the numeric value of the car chosen which is stored in E14, find it in the named area groups and return the model from the third column.

4. In G8 enter the formula: `=VLOOKUP(E14,groups,4)`

This will pick up the numeric value of the car chosen which is stored in E14, find it in the named area groups and return the insurance group from the fourth column.

These cells should now display the make, model and insurance group of the car chosen in the combo box, e.g. a Peugeot 406 is Group 10.

5. In cell G9 enter the formula:
`=LEFT(VLOOKUP(E12,Multipliers!A15:C16,2),1)`

When the option box is clicked male returns the value 1 in E12 and female returns the value 2. The **LOOKUP** function looks across to the multipliers sheet and returns Male or Female.

The **LEFT** function is used to return M and F instead of Male and Female. Clicking on Male should display a 1 in cell E12 and M in G9. If Female is selected, a 2 appears in E12 and F in G9.

6. In G10 enter the formula `=VLOOKUP(E16,Multipliers!A2:C11,2)`

The combo box which stores the age returns a value in E16. The LOOKUP function finds this value in the multipliers sheet and returns the actual age e.g. a 1 returns 17-19

7. In G11 enter the formula
`=LEFT(VLOOKUP(E18,Multipliers!A20:B22,2),1)`

The list box which stores the risk returns a value in E18. The LOOKUP function finds this value in the multipliers sheet and returns the actual risk e.g. a 1 returns a High risk area

The **LEFT** function displays the first letter of the selected risk, H, M or L.

8. In G12 enter the formula: `=IF(E22=TRUE,"Y","N")`

If the check box for the extra driver is checked E22 takes the value TRUE, if unchecked E22 takes the value FALSE. The function returns Y or N in G12.

9. In G13 enter the formula `=D24`

G13 stores the number of years no claims discount.

10. In G14 type in the formula: `=VLOOKUP(E20,Multipliers!A32:D34,4)`
   This displays the abbreviation for the insurance type in cell G14.

Your spreadsheet should appear as right.

	A	B	C	D	E	F	G
1							
2							
3							
4							
5							
6			Forename			Make	Peugeot
7			Surname			Model	406
8			Address 1			IG	10
9			Address 2			Sex	M
10			Postcode			Age	40-44
11				◉ Male		Risk	H
12			Sex	○ Female	1	Extra Driver	Y
13						No claims	4
14			Car	Peugeot 406 ▼	4	Type	FC
15							
16			Age	40-44 ▼	6		
17							
18			Area	High risk ▲	1		
19				Medium risk ▼			
20			Type	Fully comprehensive ▲	1		
21				Third party, fire & theft ▼			
22			Driver	☑ Extra Driver	TRUE		
23					Years	Percent	
24			No claims	▲	4	60%	
25				▼			

 ◄ ◄ ► ►◄ \ Groups / Multipliers \ Quotes / ◄◄

5. Preparing the quote – entering the multipliers

The next stage is to lookup and store the multiplier associated with each factor.

1. In cell H8 enter the formula: `=VLOOKUP(G8,costs,2)` This formula looks up the basic insurance cost for a car in that group, e.g. a Peugeot 406 is Group 10 and should display £264.00.

2. In cell H9 enter the formula: `=VLOOKUP(E12,Multipliers!A15:C16,3)`

   If Male is selected this cell should display 1.3. If Female is selected it displays 1. (This is because males are considered 1.3 times more likely to be in an accident than females.)

3. In cell H10 enter the formula: `=VLOOKUP(E16,Multipliers!A2:C11,3)` This displays the multiplier for that age grouping, e.g. for someone aged 40 – 44 it should display 1.2.

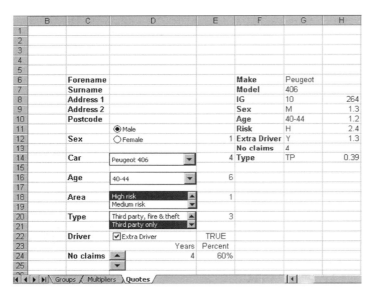

4. In cell H11 enter the formula:
   `=VLOOKUP(E18,Multipliers!A20:C22,3)`
   This displays the multiplier for the chosen risk, e.g. for a high risk area it should display 2.4.

5. In cell H12 enter the formula:
   `=IF(E22=TRUE,1.3,1)`
   This displays the multiplier for extra drivers, e.g. if the box is checked it should display 1.3.

6. In cell H14 type the formula:
   `=VLOOKUP(E20,Multipliers!A32:C34,3)`
   This displays the multiplier for the type of insurance, e.g. for a third party only it should display 0.39.

Your spreadsheet should appear as above. Note labels have been emboldened and text in column G left aligned. We will hide the multipliers later.

▶ 6. Calculating the total cost

1. Enter the headings Total without discount, No claims discount and Total cost in cells H16, H18 and H20.

2. In H16 enter `=H8*H9*H10*H11*H12*H14`

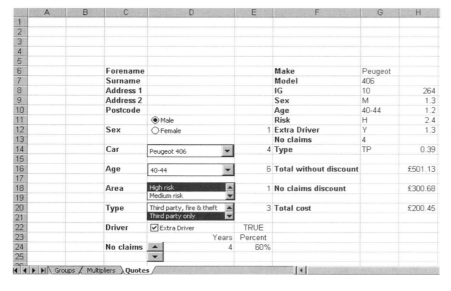

3. In H18 enter
   `=H16*E24`

4. In H20 enter
   `=H16-H18`

5. Format the totals in H16 to H20 to currency.

Your spreadsheet should appear as opposite

7. Setting up the customer worksheet

We need to set up a worksheet area to file away quotes.

1. Add a new worksheet and name it **Customers.**

2. Set the font size for the whole sheet to 8pt.

3. Set up the header row as below.

	A	B	C	D	E	F	G	H	I	J	K	L	M	N	O
1	Forename	Surname	Address1	Address2	Postcode	Make	Model	IG	Sex	Age	Risk	Extra	NCB	Type	Quote
2															

 8. Automating the filing of quotes

The system is now in a format for the user to be able to give a quote, although there is obviously a lot of work to be done yet on the screen layout.

During the development and testing of the system it is wise to leave the data in columns E and H showing. They will be hidden later.

1. We need to start by creating room on screen for the control buttons that will take the user around the system. Reduce the width of column A on the Quotes worksheet to 1.86 and B to 2.00.

This creates room to the right of the screen and starts to give the user interface a balance.

When a quote is given we will need to file it away.

We will record a macro called **Filequote** to copy the quote to the **Customers** worksheet.

This can be a very long task and needs to be done very carefully and as always should be planned and practised before recording takes place.

There are a number of ways of doing this.

2. Enter the following customer quote details including name and address:

	A	B	C	D	E	F	G	H
1								
2								
3								
4								
5								
6		**Forename**	Horace			**Make**	Ford	
7		**Surname**	Bachelor			**Model**	Fiesta	
8		**Address 1**	12 Main St			**IG**	4	194
9		**Address 2**	Derby			**Sex**	M	1.3
10		**Postcode**	DE45 6LU			**Age**	60-65	1
11			● Male			**Risk**	L	1
12		**Sex**	○ Female		1	**Extra Driver**	Y	1.3
13						**No claims**	4	
14		**Car**	Ford Fiesta ▼		7	**Type**	TP	0.39
15								
16		**Age**	60-65 ▼		10	**Total without discount**		£127.87
17								
18		**Area**	Medium risk ▲		3	**No claims discount**		£76.72
19			Low risk ▼					
20		**Type**	Third party, fire & theft ▲		3	**Total cost**		£51.15
21			Third party only ▼					
22		**Driver**	☑ Extra Driver	TRUE				
23				Years	Percent			
24		**No claims**	▲	4	60%			
25			▼					

◄ ◄ ► ►◄ \ Groups / Multipliers \ **Quotes** / Customers / Printed Quote / Data / | ◄ |

▢ Method 1

1. Insert a new worksheet and name it **Data**.

The purpose of the sheet is to act as a temporary store for the data entered in the quotes worksheet.

2. Set up the worksheet with headings and formulas as shown. Set the font size to 8 pt.

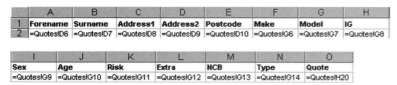

	A	B	C	D	E	F	G	H
1	Forename	Surname	Address1	Address2	Postcode	Make	Model	IG
2	=Quotes!D6	=Quotes!D7	=Quotes!D8	=Quotes!D9	=Quotes!D10	=Quotes!G6	=Quotes!G7	=Quotes!G8

	I	J	K	L	M	N	O
	Sex	Age	Risk	Extra	NCB	Type	Quote
	=Quotes!G9	=Quotes!G10	=Quotes!G11	=Quotes!G12	=Quotes!G13	=Quotes!G14	=Quotes!H20

The data will look like this:

	A	B	C	D	E	F	G	H	I	J	K	L	M	N	O
1	Forename	Surname	Address1	Address2	Postcode	Make	Model	IG	Sex	Age	Risk	Extra	NCB	Type	Quote
2	Horace	Bachelor	12 Main St	Derby	DE45 6LU	Ford	Fiesta	4	M	60-65	L	Y	4	TP	51.15

When a new quote is made the data is automatically picked up on this worksheet.

This row of data then needs copying and pasting to the customers worksheet.

The steps in the macro are:

1. Start recording.

2. Switch to the **Customers** worksheet.

3. Select row 2 and insert a row.

4. Switch to the **Data** worksheet.

5. Select cells A2 to O2 and click **Copy**.

6. Switch to the **Customers** sheet.

7. Select cell A2 and click **Edit**, **Paste Special, Values** and click **OK**.

8. Click on a free space in the spreadsheet area.

9. Stop recording.

We will design a button to run the macro later.

Method 2

The second method involves moving groups of data from the **Quotes** worksheet to an area on the **Customer** worksheet using copy and paste.

We need to move the name and address, the data in column G and the total cost in cell H20.

We will copy and paste the data to column P on the **Customer** worksheet, then move each item into its correct cell using copy and paste again.

The process will appear something like the screen image below but we will record the macro so that the contents of column P are deleted.

	A	B	C	D	E	F	G	H	I	J	K	L	M	N	O	P
1	Forename	Surname	Address1	Address2	Postcode	Make	Model	IG	Sex	Age	Risk	Extra	NCB	Type	Qoute	
2	Horace	Bachelor	12 Main St	Derby	DE45 6LU	Ford	Fiesta	4	M	60-65	L	Y		4	TP	£51.15 Horace
3																Bachelor
4																12 Main St
5																Derby
6																DE45 6LU
7																Ford
8																Fiesta
9																4
10																M
11																60-65
12																L
13																Y
14																4
15																TP
16																£51.15

Note

- The cells in column G and cell H20 contain formulas. Therefore **Edit**, **Paste Special, Values** must be used so that only the values in the cells are copied and not the formulae.

Method 3

Alternatively it is possible to copy slowly and carefully in turn each item from the **Customers** worksheet to the **Quotes** worksheet. This involves very many steps and is clearly prone to error.

This is not recommended but is certainly acceptable.

9. Clearing the current screen to enter a new quote

When the quote has been filed away we need to clear the screen ready for a new quote.

We will record a macro called **Clearscreen** to carry out the process.

As always, plan and practise the macro before recording.

There is a difficulty with this process. It is not just a case of selecting cells and clicking **Edit, Clear, All.**

A number of the cells contain complex formulas and we do not wish to clear them from the spreadsheet.

When recording the macro we need to clear the name and address in D6 to D10 and simply delete the numbers returned by the various controls in column E.

The steps are:

1. Switch to the **Quotes** worksheet.

2. Start recording.

3. Highlight cells D6 to D10.

4. From the menu click on **Edit, Clear, All.**

5. Highlight cells E12 to E22 and click on **Edit, Clear, Contents**.

6. Highlight cell D24 and click on **Edit, Clear, Contents**.

7. Return the cursor to cell D6.

8. Stop recording

9. Test the macro

The macro should clear the data and place the cursor in position for the next quote.

Add a button to run the macro on the **Quotes** worksheet in cells F23 and F24.

Improving the screen layout (optional)

At the same time you will notice errors in column G because the functions contained in the cells have nothing to work on. You can leave this, the system will still work as soon as data is entered but it is messy.

In situations like this it is not uncommon to format the font in the cells to white.

However we are going to hide the values in column G a little more professionally.

If any position in the data entry area of the worksheet, i.e. cells in column D and E, is blank then errors will appear in column G.

We will use an **IF** statement to detect blank cells in the data entry area and replace the errors generated with a blank. If cells in the data entry area do not contain a blank then the functions in column G will operate as normal.

Enter the formulas as shown below. Use of copy and paste may help.

	F	G	H
1			
2			
3			
4			
5			
6	Make	=IF(E14="","",VLOOKUP(E14,Groups,2))	
7	Model	=IF(E14="","",VLOOKUP(E14,Groups,3))	
8	IG	=IF(E14="","",VLOOKUP(E14,Groups,4))	=IF(G8="","",VLOOKUP(G8,Costs,2))
9	Sex	=IF(E12="","",LEFT(VLOOKUP(E12,Multipliers!A15:C16,2),1))	=IF(E12="","",VLOOKUP(E12,Multipliers!A15:C16,3))
10	Age	=IF(E16="","",VLOOKUP(E16,Multipliers!A2:C11,2))	=IF(E16="","",VLOOKUP(E16,Multipliers!A2:C11,3))
11	Risk	=IF(E18="","",LEFT(VLOOKUP(E18,Multipliers!A20:B22,2),1))	=IF(E18="","",VLOOKUP(E18,Multipliers!A20:C22,3))
12	Extra Driver	=IF(E22="","",LEFT(IF(E22=TRUE,"Yes","No"),1))	=IF(E22="","",IF(E22=TRUE,1.3,1))
13	No claims	=IF(D24="","",D24)	
14	Type	=IF(E20="","",VLOOKUP(E20,Multipliers!A32:D34,4))	=IF(E20="","",VLOOKUP(E20,Multipliers!A32:C34,3))
15			
16	Total without discount		=IF(D6="","",H8*H9*H10*H11*H12*H14)
17			
18	No claims discount		=IF(D6="","",H16*E24)
19			
20	Total cost		=IF(D6="","",H16-H18)

The formula in E24 also needs changing to
=IF(D24="","",VLOOKUP(D24,Multipliers!B25:C29,2))   .

The same process is used in cells H8 to H14. These figures are not needed on screen and simply formatting the font to white is another option.

		C	D	E	F	G	H	I	J
2									
3									
4									
5									
6		Forename	Peter		Make	Ford			
7		Surname	Williams		Model	Fiesta			
8		Address 1	97 Arthur St		IG	4	194		
9		Address 2	Derby		Sex	M	1.3		
10		Postcode	DE65 6RT		Age	45-49	1.15		
11			⦿ Male		Risk	M	1.7		
12		Sex	○ Female	1	Extra Driver	Y	1.3		
13					No claims	3			
14		Car	Ford Fiesta ▼	7	Type	FC	1		
15									
16		Age	45-49 ▼	7	Total without discount		£640.97		
17									
18		Area	Medium risk ▲	2	No claims discount		£320.48		
19			Low risk ▼						
20		Type	Fully comprehensive ▲	1	Total cost		£320.48		
21			Third party, fire & theft ▼						
22		Driver	☑ Extra Driver		TRUE				
23				Years	Percent	Clear Screen			
24		No claims	▲	3	50%				
25			▼						

▶ 10. Designing the printed quote

The next stage is to design the layout of the printed quote and set it up to take the data from the **Quotes** worksheet.

1. Insert a new sheet by right clicking one of the sheet tabs and choosing insert. Rename it **Printed Quote**.

2. Set up rows 1 to 8 to display the letterhead as shown below.

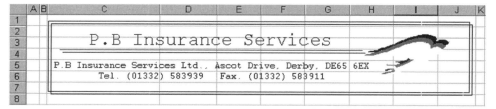

The header is made up of the following using the **Drawing** toolbar in Excel.

⫸ Column A and B are closed down to width 2.

⫸ A Text box containing P.B Insurance Services Ltd., Courier New font size 20pt.

⫸ A Text box containing the address in Courier font size 8pt.

⫸ A double line and a double border.

⫸ A logo of a bluebird.

⫸ A thin line is inserted around the quote information.

3. Set up rows 11 to 36 to display the headings and formulas as shown below.

The formulas link to the **Quotes** worksheet and display the quote data

	A	B	C	D
11			Date	=TODAY()
12				
13			Insurance Quotation for:	
14				
15			=Quotes!D6&" "&Quotes!D7	
16			=Quotes!D8	
17			=Quotes!D9	
18			=Quotes!D10	
19				
20			Make	=Quotes!G6
21			Model	=Quotes!G7
22			Age	=Quotes!G10
23			Sex	=IF(Quotes!G9="M",'Male',"Female")
24			Extra Driver	=IF(Quotes!G12="Y" "Yes","No")
25			Insurance type	=VLOOKUP(Quotes!E18,Multipliers!A32:B34,2)
26			Years no claims bonus	=Quotes!G13
27				
28			Quotation	=Quotes!H20
29				
30			Quotation valid to	=TODAY()+14
31				
32			Signed on behalf of PB Insurance Services Ltd	
33				
34				
35				
36			Paul Bryant, Managing Director	

4. Finally remove the gridlines.

11. Adding user options to the quotes screen

We need to offer the following options on the quotes screen.

- File a quote.
- Print a quote.
- View quotes.
- Edit groups.
- Edit multipliers.
- Exit

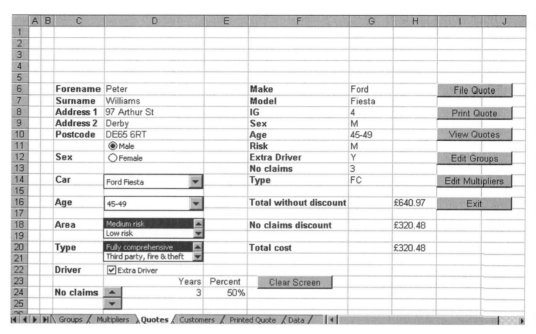

Macros need to be set up to automate each option and a button added to each macro.

Remember to practise and plan the steps before recording each macro.

File a quote

This macro has already been recorded in stage 8. All we need to do is add a button to run it.

1. From the menu **View, Toolbars, Form,** drag out a button across I6 and J6. Click after the text and name it **File Quote**.

2. Right button click will call up the **Format** menu. Select **Assign macro**, choose the macro **Filequote** and click **OK**.

Print a quote

We need to record a macro to print the quote. Call the macro **Printquote**.

The steps are:

1. Start recording.

2. Switch to the **Printed Quote** sheet by clicking its tab.

3. From the menu choose **File**, **Print** and click **OK**.

4. Click on the **Quotes** tab to return to the **Quotes** sheet.

5. Stop recording.

6. Add a button to the quotes sheet by dragging a button across cells I8 and J8. Name it **Print Quote**.

View quotes

This is a simple macro called **viewquotes** which will switch from the **Quotes** sheet to the **Customers** sheet.

The steps are:

1. Start recording.

2. Click on the **Customers** worksheet.

3. Stop recording.

4. Add a button to cells I10 and J10 of the **Quotes** worksheet and call it **View Quotes**.

Edit groups

In exactly the same way as above, record a macro to move to the **Groups** worksheet and position the button across cells I12 and J12 of the **Quotes** worksheet. Label the button **Edit Groups** and call the macro **editgroups**.

Edit multipliers

In exactly the same way, record a macro to move to the **Multipliers** worksheet and position the button across cells I14 and J14 of the **Quotes** worksheet. Label the button **Edit Multipliers** and call the macro **editmultipliers**.

Exit

Position the button across cells I16 and J16. We will set up the macro later.

To link the system together macros need to be recorded to return
the user from each of the **Groups**, the **Multipliers** and the
Customers worksheets. Name the macro **Quotes** and attach a
button to it labelled **Return to Quotes** in an appropriate place on
each worksheet.

12. Customising the interface and some finishing touches

Your system should now be working and appear as below.

Forename Peter		**Make**	Ford	File Quote
Surname Williams		**Model**	Fiesta	
Address 1 97 Arthur St		**IG**	4	Print Quote
Address 2 Derby		**Sex**	M	
Postcode DE65 6RT		**Age**	45-49	View Quotes
⦿ Male		**Risk**	M	
Sex ○ Female		**Extra Driver**	Y	Edit Groups
		No claims	3	
Car Ford Fiesta		**Type**	FC	Edit Multipliers
Age 45-49		**Total without discount**		£640.97 Exit
Area Medium risk / Low risk		**No claims discount**		£320.48
Type Fully comprehensive / Third party, fire & theft		**Total cost**		£320.48
Driver ☑ Extra Driver				
No claims Years 3 Percent 50%	Clear Screen			

Groups / Multipliers / **Quotes** / Customers / Printed Quote / Data

You can ignore this section and move to section 13 but with clever use of lines, boxes, colour fills and a smart logo, it is possible to transform the look and feel of your system interface to the one below.

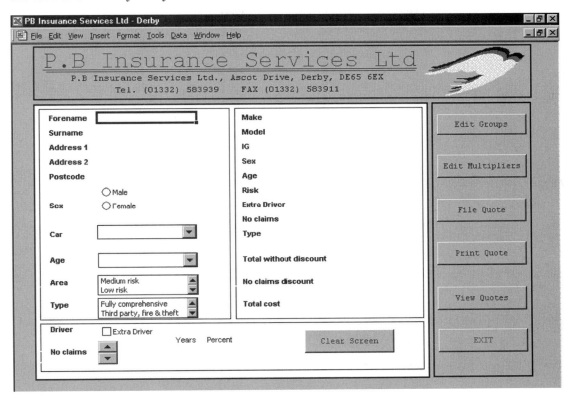

Adding the auto_open macro

When Excel loads it looks to see if an **auto_open** macro is present. If it is, it is executed.

We want our system to load without the appearance of a spreadsheet by removing the gridlines, sheet tabs, row and column headings etc.

We will record a macro called **auto_open**.

The steps are:

1. Start recording.

2. Click **Tools, Options**.

3. Uncheck the gridlines, row and column headings, sheet tabs, scroll bars.

4. Uncheck the **Formula bar** and **Status bar** and click on **OK**.

5. Click **View, Toolbars** and remove the **Standard** and **Formatting Toolbars** (if present).

6. Stop recording.

Click **Tools, Macro, Visual Basic Editor** to view your macro code.

```
Sub auto_open()
`

` auto_open Macro
` Macro recorded 20/10/2000
`

`

    With ActiveWindow

Application.Caption = "PB Insurance Services Ltd"

        .DisplayGridlines = False
        .DisplayHeadings = False
        .DisplayHorizontalScrollBar = False
        .DisplayVerticalScrollBar = False
        .DisplayWorkbookTabs = False
    End With
    With Application
        .DisplayFormulaBar = False
        .DisplayStatusBar = False
    End With
    Application.CommandBars("Standard").Visible = False
    Application.CommandBars("Formatting").Visible = False
End Sub
```

Insert the line *Application.Caption = "PB Insurance Services Ltd"* as shown and change your filename to Derby. This code replaces the Microsoft Excel header as shown below.

Adding the auto_close macro

When we close our system down, Excel looks to run an **auto_close** macro if present.

On leaving the system we want to restore Excel's original settings.

We will record a macro called **auto_close**. The steps are:

1. Start recording.

2. Click on **Tools, Options**.

3. Check the gridlines, row and column headings, sheet tabs, scroll bars.

4. Check the **Formula bar** and **Status bar** and click on **OK**.

5. Click **View, Toolbars** and restore the **Standard** and **Formatting Tool**bars.

6. Stop recording.

Click **Tools, Macro, Visual Basic Editor** to view your macro code.

```
Sub auto_close()

`
`   auto_close Macro
`   Macro recorded 20/10/2000
`


`

    With ActiveWindow
        .DisplayGridlines = True
        .DisplayHeadings = True
        .DisplayHorizontalScrollBar = True
        .DisplayVerticalScrollBar = True
        .DisplayWorkbookTabs = True
    End With
    With Application
        .DisplayFormulaBar = True
        .DisplayStatusBar = True
    End With
    Application.CommandBars("Standard").Visible = True
    Application.CommandBars("Formatting").Visible = True
End Sub
```

The macro as it stands merely restores the Excel settings , we want to save and close our application down. If you have added an application caption we also need to remove that.

Add the following lines before the End Sub

```
Application.Caption = Empty
ActiveWorkbook.Saved = True
Application.Quit
```

These lines of code clear the caption, save the current workbook and close down Excel.

13. Adding a Front End

The last stage is to add the front end below to the system.

The **Exit** button will close down the system, **Enter** will move to the **Quotes** interface and the **About** button will give system details.

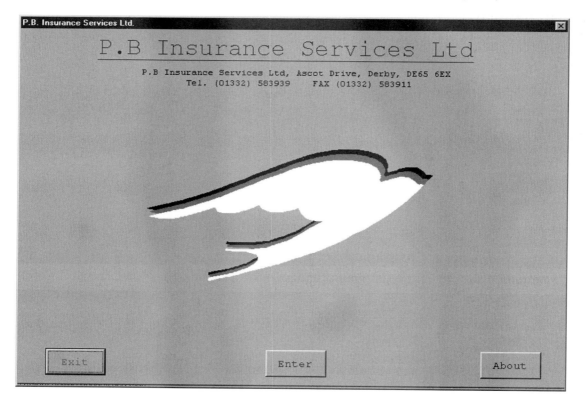

1. Load the Visual Basic Editor by clicking on **Tools, Macro, Visual Basic Editor**.

2. Click on **Insert, UserForm**.

3. Using the **Text Box** and **Image** tools design a suitable **Front End**.

4. In the **Properties Window** for the **User Form** set the **Caption** to P.B Insurance Services Ltd., the **Height** to 420 and **Width** to 600.

5. Set the **Zoom** property to about 65 to make it easier to view.

6. Add three **Command Buttons**. By default they are called CommandButton1,2 and 3. Edit the button labels to **Exit**, **Enter** and **About**.

7. Right click on the **User Form** and click **View Code**.

The window below will appear. It is now just a case of tinkering with the code.

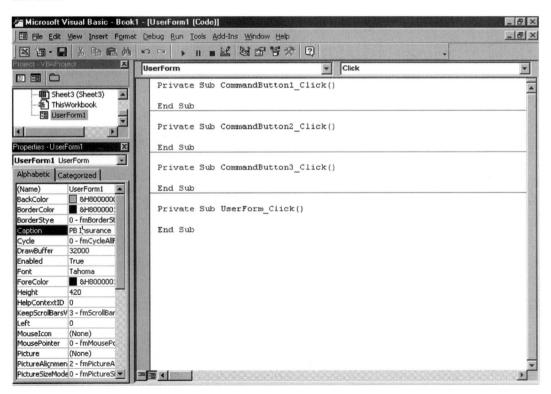

Enter these lines of code for each button between the Sub and End Sub.

The **Exit** button (closes the system down).

```
Private Sub CommandButton1_Click()
Application.Quit
End Sub
```

The **Enter** button (hides the User Form and runs a macro called Start).

```
Private Sub CommandButton2_Click()
UserForm1.Hide
Start
End Sub
```

The **About** button (runs a Message box).

```
Private Sub CommandButton3_Click()
MsgBox "Advanced Projects in Excel by Mott and Rendell", vbOKOnly, "P.B Insurance Services"
End Sub
```

We also need to make a few changes to our **auto_open** macro. We now want it to load the User Form. When we select enter on the User Form we want to remove the user form and then run a macro called Start which effectively runs the original auto_open macro.

Edit the macro as shown below.

NB. The command `ScreenUpdating = False` can be used to reduce the screen flicker.

```
Sub auto_open()

`  auto`open Macro
`  Macro recorded 20/10/2000 by JPS



Load UserForm1
UserForm1.Show

End Sub

Sub start()

Application.Caption = "P.B Insurance Services Ltd"

    With ActiveWindow
        .DisplayGridlines = False
        .DisplayHeadings = False
        .DisplayHorizontalScrollBar = False
        .DisplayVerticalScrollBar = False
        .DisplayWorkbookTabs = False
    End With
    With Application
        .DisplayFormulaBar = False
        .DisplayStatusBar = False
    End With
    Application.CommandBars("Standard").Visible = False
    Application.CommandBars("Formatting").Visible = False
    Range("D6").Select

End Sub
```

Finally, test the system thoroughly. When you are satisfied that it is
fully working, add cell protection where appropriate.

Documenting the car insurance quotation system

Documenting a system

An ICT project is much more than just setting up the system using Microsoft Excel. You must also include documentation covering the analysis of the system, its design, its implementation, testing, a user guide and evaluation.

The following pages show you how to document your system by looking at some of the documentation provided with the P.B Insurance Services Ltd system.

Remember: This documentation is not complete but each section offers examples, pointers and hints to what is considered good practice.

P.B Insurance Services Ltd Car Insurance Quotes

Contents

1. Specification

(a) Introduction

(b) Resources Available

(c) End-User Requirements

    (i)   Input requirements
    (ii) Processing requirements
    (iii) Output requirements

(d) Designs

(e) Sub-tasks

(f) Test plan

2. Implementation Report

3. Testing

(a) Test results

(b) User testing

4. User guide

5. Evaluation report

■ 1. Specification

In this section you need to give some of the background to your proposed system and its requirements.

□ (a) Introduction

Paul Bryant runs a small car insurance brokers.

He works full-time from his Derby office. He has a part-time assistant who tends to work evenings and weekends.

He has developed a loyal customer base who regularly ring the office when car insurance renewal is due. To maintain customer relations and develop his business by attracting new clients, he often conducts business at the home of his customers.

To calculate the insurance quote Paul uses his calculator and a table of insurance ratings.

All cars are allocated to an insurance group (IG) number. The more expensive and powerful the car, the higher the rating e.g. a Ford Puma is IG 9.

■ INSURANCE GROUP COSTS

IG	Basic Cost
1	£ 174.00
2	£ 180.00
3	£ 187.00
4	£ 194.00
5	£ 202.00
6	£ 210.00
7	£ 222.00
8	£ 235.00
9	£ 248.00

10	£ 264.00
11	£ 280.00
12	£ 300.00
...	...

The insurance group basic price is then adjusted according to a range of criteria.

The younger you are the more you are considered a risk and hence the more you pay. For example, a person aged 20-24 has a factor of 2.4.

So a 21 year old driving a Ford Puma would pay £248 x 2.4 = £595.20.

■ AGE FACTORS

Age	Multiplier
17-19	4.80
20-24	2.40
25-29	2.00
30-34	1.50
35-39	1.30
40-44	1.20
45-49	1.15
50-54	1.10
55-59	1.05
60-65	1.00

Age is not the only factor that comes into play.

If you are male you are considered a higher risk than if you are female by a factor of 1.3.

Hence if the 21 year old driver of the Ford Puma was male he would pay £248 x 2.4 x 1.3 = £773.36

▪ SEX FACTORS

Sex	Multiplier
Male	1.30
Female	1.00

Other factors that are taken into account are the type of area you live in which is classified as high, medium or low risk.

▪ AREA FACTORS

Area	Multiplier
High risk	2.40
Medium risk	1.70
Low risk	1.00

Insurance types available are third party, third party fire and theft, and fully comprehensive.

▪ INSURANCE TYPE FACTORS

Type	Multiplier	Abbreviation
Fully comprehensive	1	FC
Third party, fire & theft	0.46	TPFT
Third party only	0.39	TP

An extra driver can be added to the policy by adding a factor of 1.3.

No claims discount is available as the table below shows:

▪ NO CLAIMS DISCOUNTS

No Claim Bonus	Multiplier
0	0%
1	30%
2	40%

3	50%
4	60%

Paul more than often is issuing his quotes over the phone. It is quite a lengthy process using his calculator and reference tables and quotes are handwritten or word-processed which in turn is lengthy. He would like to automate the system and make better use of his PC. When he makes customer visits, he would like to be able to take a laptop computer for the purpose of issuing quotes.

(b) Resources Available

In the office Paul has a Pentium II with 64Mb of memory. The operating system is Windows 98 and the Office 2000 suite is installed including Excel 2000. He has a powerful Epson Laser printer for high quality printing.

He also has available an older laptop, Pentium 200 with 32Mb of memory, Office 2000 is installed but it runs slowly. It is not advisable nor practical to move the laser printer around so out of office work can only be done on screen.

Working between the two machines will require careful attention to transferring and backing up files between each machine.

Paul and his assistant are reasonably competent with the day-to-day use of a PC and will only need simple instructions to get started.

(c) End-User Requirements

1. A system is required to be able to give a quick quote accurately and efficiently.
2. The system must produce multiple copies of the quote.
3. The system should enable phone enquiries to be dealt with far more quickly than at present.
4. Issued quotes need to be stored with the facility to view at a later date.
5. Quotes should be issued with a professional look on letter-headed paper.
6. The system must be user friendly, yet have a professional look and feel.
7. The system should be easy to transfer easily between the laptop and office-based PC.

■ (i)   INPUT REQUIREMENTS

Customer details to include:

- forename;
- surname;
- address;
- sex;
- make and model of car;
- age of driver in grouped format e.g. 40-45;
- type of insurance, fully comprehensive, third party fire and theft or third party;
- area risk assessment given as high, medium or low;
- extra driver to be declared or not;
- no claims discount up to a maximum of 60% for 4 years no claims;

Insurance details to include:

- insurance group ratings for makes of cars;
- multiplying factors to be allocated to sex, age of driver, area risk and insurance type.

■ (ii)   PROCESSING REQUIREMENTS

- Details of insurance group will be looked up from a table.
- Details of multiplying factors to be used will be looked up from a table.
- Data will be transferred from the client details area on screen to the customers area.
- The cost of the quote will be calculated with and without discount.
- Quote details will be stored for future reference.

■ (iii)   OUTPUT REQUIREMENTS

- Full quote details on screen.
- Fully customised and professionally printed output with company logo and header.

(d) Design

The project should be broken down into clear sub-tasks or modules, which should relate to the users requirements. Produce design plans for each sub-task.

Your design plans should be done away from the computer.

Design plans are probably best done by hand. You could use A3 paper and/or use a blank grid from an Excel spreadsheet.

Good spreadsheet designs will include details of:

- sheet naming, named cells and cell ranges;
- validation and cell protection;
- labels and formulae used;
- links between sheets;
- general sheet layouts;
- interfaces and screen designs;
- macros and macro buttons;
- any customised outputs.

(e) Sub-tasks

I will break the car insurance problem down into the following sub-tasks

1. **The Insurance Groups worksheet**

2. The Multipliers worksheet

3. **The Quotes worksheet**
   (a) customer details section
   (b) quote details section
   (c) the calculation

4. The Customers worksheet

5. Macros are needed to:
   (a) file the quotes
   (b) clear the screen

6. The printed quote worksheet

7. **The Start-up screen and options**

The designs for the sub-tasks highlighted in bold are shown on pages 143–146:

■ SUB TASK 1 DESIGN

The Insurance Groups worksheet

	A	B	C	D	E	F	G	H	I
1	Number	Make	Model	19	CarName			19	BasicCost
2	1							1	174
3	2							2	180
4	3							3	...
5	4							4	
6	5							5	
7	6	FORD	KA	2	FORD KA			6	
8	7							7	
9	...							...	
10					Groups				Costs
11									
12									
13									
14									
15									
16									
17									
18									
19									
20									
21	20							20	
22									
23									

Column H stores the insurance group from 1 to 20.

Column I stores the basic cost for each group, formatted to currency.

The range of cells from H1 to I21 is named 'Costs.'

Column A has the code number for each car, e.g. 6 = Ford Ka.

Column B stores the make

Column C stores the model

Column D store the insurance group

Column E calculates the full name of the car using concatenation

e.g. = B7 & " " & C7

The range of cells from A1 to E21 is named 'Groups'

The worksheet will also need a button to run the Quotes macro to return to the Quotes worksheet.

Worksheet will be named Groups

SUB TASK 3 DESIGN 1

The Quotes worksheet

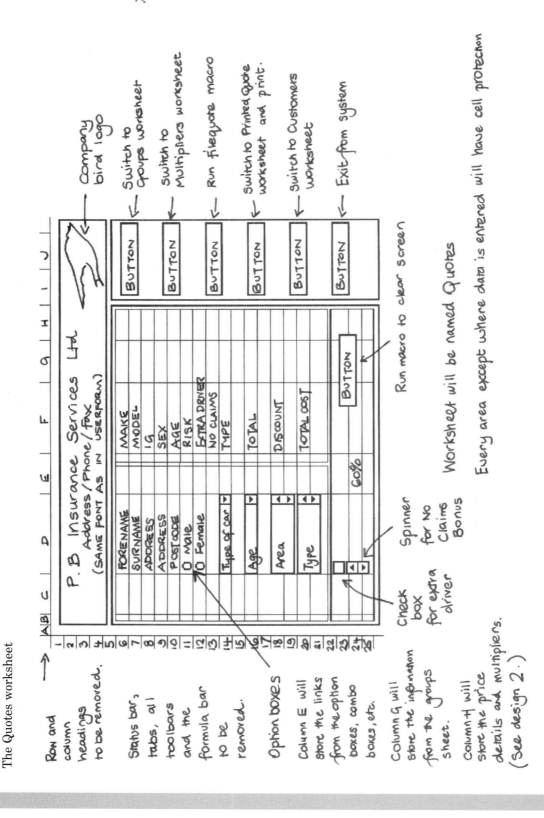

Row and column headings to be removed.

Status bar, tabs, all toolbars and the formula bar to be removed.

Option boxes

Column E will store the links from the option boxes, combo boxes, etc.

Column G will store the information from the groups sheet.

Column H will store the price details and multipliers. (See design 2.)

Company bird logo

Switch to Groups worksheet

Switch to Multipliers worksheet

Run fileqote macro

Switch to Printed Quote worksheet and print.

Switch to Customers worksheet

Exit from system

Check box for extra driver

Spinner for No Claims Bonus

Run macro to clear screen

Worksheet will be named Quotes

Every area except where data is entered will have cell protection

P. B Insurance Services Ltd
Address / Phone / Fax
(SAME FONT AS IN USERFORM)

FORENAME   MAKE
SURNAME   MODEL
ADDRESS   IG
POSTCODE   SEX
O Male   AGE
O Female   RISK
            EXTRA DRIVER
            NO CLAIMS
Type of car TYPE

Age   TOTAL

Area   DISCOUNT

Type   TOTAL COST

            60%

■ SUB TASK 3 DESIGN 2

The Quotes worksheet in close up

	D	E	F	G	H
6	Forename entered here		Make	e.g. Ford	
7	Surname		Model	e.g. Ka	
8	Address 1		Insurance Group	e.g. 2	e.g. 180
9	Address 2		Sex	F	1
10	Postcode		Age	25-29	2
11	⊙ Male option box	1 if male	Risk	M	1.7
12	⊙ Female option box	2 if female	Extra driver	Y	1.3
13			No claims	4	
14	Car combo box ▶	Car code e.g. 15	Type	FC	1
15					
16	Age combo box ▶	age code e.g. 3	Total without discount		TOTAL
17					
18	Area list box ◀▶	1, 2 or 3	No claims discount		DISCOUNT
19					
20	Type list box ◀▶	1, 2 or 3	Total cost		TOTAL
21					
22	☑ Extra driver check box	TRUE/FALSE			
23					
24	◀ No of years	% discount			
25	▶ No claims spinner				

Use VLOOKUP on groups worksheet to display Make, Model and I.G.

Use VLOOKUP to find Basic cost.

Cells G9 to G14 use VLOOKUP to display information.

Cells H9 to H12 and H14 use VLOOKUP to find multipliers. They are coloured white as this information does not need to be displayed.

In H16 the total is calculated using the formula:
= H8 * H9 * H10 * H11 * H12 * H14

In H18 the no claims discount is calculated using the formula:
= H16 * E24

In H20 the final total is = H16 − H18

Every area except where data is entered will have cell protection

Text in cells E12 to E22 is coloured white so that it is not displayed.

Gridlines turned off.

Worksheet will be named Quotes

■ SUB TASK 5B DESIGN

Macro to clear the screen (after quote has been filed)

The macro must:

1. select the Quotes worksheet;

2. select cells D6 to D10;

3. clear these cells;

4. select cells E12, E14, E16, E18, E20, E22 and D24 (using CTRL and click);

5. clear the contents.

■ SUB TASK 7 DESIGN

The Start-up screen and options

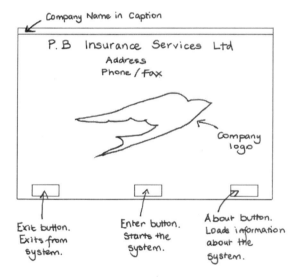

Company Name in Caption

P. B Insurance Services Ltd
Address
Phone / Fax

Company logo

Exit button. Exits from system.

Enter button. Starts the system.

About button. Loads information about the system.

Design do's
- Present your plans in a format such that a reasonably competent person could take them and make a start on setting up your system.
- Make them legible and neat. This person must be able read them.

Design don'ts
- Don't use screen dumps from the actual system as part of your design plans

(f) Test plan

Testing is an integral part of developing an IT system and your design should include a test plan, saying exactly what you will test and how.

Tests should:

- be numbered;
- state the purpose of the test;
- specify the data to be used, if any;
- outline the expected result;
- cross-reference to clear hard copy usually in the form of a screen dump;
- provide evidence of the actual results plus any comments;
- outline any corrective action needed or taken.

Test data should include typical data and if possible, extreme, invalid or awkward data.

■ THE INSURANCE GROUPS WORKSHEET

Test Number	Purpose of Test	Test Data Used	Expected Outcome and Comments	Actual Outcome
1	Test the CONC function in column E combines contents of columns B and C	All makes and models in named range Groups	Make and Model combined with space in between	

■ SETTING UP THE QUOTES WORKSHEET –

Testing the input controls for entering the driver details

Test Number	Purpose of Test	Test Data Used	Expected Outcome	Actual Outcome and Comments
2	Test Option buttons (Sex)	Click on male/female	Returns 1 or 2 in E12	
3	Test Combo box (Car) returns correct values	Ford Ka	Returns 6 in E14	
4	Test Combo box (Age) returns correct values	60-65	Returns 10 in E16	

5	Test Area List box returns correct values	Low risk	Returns 3 in E18
6	Test Type List box returns correct values	Fully comprehensive	Returns 1 in E20
7	Test Check box returns TRUE/FALSE	Check the check box and uncheck it	Returns TRUE/FALSE in E22
8	Test the Spinner control and LOOKUP returns correct discount	Increment spinner to 2 years	40% should be looked up and returned in E24

■ PREPARING THE QUOTES –

Testing the VLOOKUP and other functions

Test Number	Purpose of Test	Test Data Used	Expected Outcome	Actual Outcome and Comments
9	Test VLOOKUP in G6, G7, G8 returns correct values from the named range Groups	Peugeot 406 is chosen from D14 returning 4 in E14	Car details and IG returned in G6, G7, G8 - Peugeot 406 IG 10	
10	Test VLOOKUP in G10 and G14 returns correct values from the named worksheet Multipliers	Age 40-44 Type Fully comprehensive	40-44 and FC returned in G10 and G14	
11	Test VLOOKUP+LEFT function in G9, G11 returns correct values from the worksheet Multipliers.	Choose Male and High Risk	First letters M and H returned in G9 and G11	
12	Test IF function in G12 returns correct value	Check Extra driver in E22	Y is returned in G12	
13	Test no-claims discount is transferred from D24 to G13	Increment spinner to 4 years	4 years is returned in G13	

▓ PREPARING THE QUOTES –

Entering the multipliers for calculating the total cost

Test Number	Purpose of Test	Test Data Used	Expected Outcome	Actual Outcome and Comments
14	Test the multipliers are looked up correctly from the worksheet named Multipliers	Select Peugeot 406	H8 should return £264	
		Enter sex male	H9 should return 1.3	
		Enter age 40-44	H10 should return 1.2	
		Select High Risk	H11 should return 2.4	
		Choose Third Party Insurance	H14 should return 0.39	
		Choose Extra driver	H12 should return 1.3	

▓ CALCULATING THE TOTAL COST OF THE QUOTE

Test Number	Purpose of Test	Test Data Used	Expected Outcome	Actual Outcome and Comments
15	Test the formulas H16, H18 and H20 calculate bill correctly	Data for Test 14 above	Bill worked out on calculator. Total cost = £200.45	

▓ AUTOMATING THE FILING OF QUOTES

Test Number	Purpose of Test	Test Data Used	Expected Outcome	Actual Outcome and Comments
16	Test the macro 'filequote' to see if data is transferred correctly to the Customers worksheet	Routine data ie.short name and address plus car details	On running the macro, details should appear in the customer sheet	
	Test the macro 'filequote' to see if data is transferred correctly to the Customers worksheet and within the column widths set	Routine data BUT a longer name and address plus car details	On running the macro, details should appear in the customer sheet	
	Test the macro 'filequote' when no data is entered	No data entered	A blank row should appear in the customer sheet	

■ CLEARING THE CURRENT SCREEN TO ENTER A NEW QUOTE

Test Number	Purpose of Test	Test Data Used	Expected Outcome	Actual Outcome and Comments
17	Test macro 'clear screen' after Start up	Routine driver and car details	Screen should be clear	
	Test macro 'clear screen' after a quote has been filed	Routine driver and car details	Screen should be clear	
	Test macro 'clear screen' after it has been run once	No data	Screen should be clear	

■ PRINTING THE QUOTE

Test Number	Purpose of Test	Test Data Used	Expected Outcome	Actual Outcome and Comments
18	Test details are taken from the Quotes sheet to the Printed quote worksheet sheet	Normal driver and car details	Details display correctly on the Printed quote sheet	

■ ADDING THE USER OPTIONS

Test Number	Purpose of Test	Test Data Used	Expected Outcome	Actual Outcome and Comments
19	Test Print Quote	Test macro button	Prints quote	
20	Test View Quotes	Test macro button	Moves to Customers sheet	
21	Test Edit Groups	Test macro button	Moves to Groups worksheet	
22	Test Edit Multipliers	Test macro button	Moves to Multipliers sheet	
23	Test links to the other worksheets and the return options	Test the macro buttons	Be able to switch to chosen sheet and back to quotes worksheet	

■ CUSTOMISING THE INTERFACE AND FINISHING TOUCHES

Test Number	Purpose of Test	Test Data Used	Expected Outcome	Actual Outcome and Comments
24	Test the auto_open macro starts the system correctly	Start the system up	System loads and removes Excel standard features	
25	Test the auto_close macro closes down the system properly	Close the system down	System closes and restores Excel standard features	

■ ADDING THE FRONT END AND FURTHER OPTIONS

Test Number	Purpose of Test	Test Data Used	Expected Outcome	Actual Outcome and Comments
26	Test again the auto_open macro	Start the system up	System loads Front End screen	
27	Test the About macro button	None, test macro button	On screen help message given	
28	Test the Exit macro button	None, test macro button	System closes down	
29	Test the Enter macro button	None, test macro button	Quotes screen loads	

■ USER TESTING

Text Number	Purpose of Test	Actual Outcome and Comments
30	Install the system in the office at PB Insurance for a week for Paul Bryant and his assistant to see if it meets his requirements.	

Testing do's

■ To find errors you have to try and provoke failure. Try to make your system go wrong!

■ Remember that you are testing whether the data is processed correctly, not just whether a button works or not.

Testing dont's

■ Don't forget. The purpose of testing is to find errors.

■ The **end user** should also be involved in testing or if there is not a real end-user get a colleague to go through your system.

■ You could use a questionnaire and analyse the results.

■ They may comment on:

　■ its ease of use

　■ consistencies of layout, fonts, buttons, colours used

　■ look and feel of the interface

　■ simple vocabulary, spelling, and grammar used

■ Implementation

This section should contain clear evidence that you have implemented each part of your system.

Screen dumps and/or printouts need to be used to support and provide evidence of work done. Where you have used formulas include a print-out or screen shot showing the formulas.

At the end of the section, explain why you have used each of the features used in your projects, e.g. 'I have used a macro to file quotes because a complicated, frequently-used task is reduced to one click of the mouse'.

■ 2. Implementation Report

In setting up the system, I have done the following tasks

A **Set up the Insurance Groups worksheet with details of cars and insurance groups.**

B Set up the Multipliers worksheet.

C **Set up the Quotes worksheet with the input controls to enter the driver details.**

D Set up the Quotes worksheet by setting up the LOOKUP functions to bring in the quote data.

E **Set up the Quotes worksheet by entering the multipliers to be used in calculating the quote.**

F Calculated the total cost of the quote.

G Set up the Customer worksheet to store details of quotes issued.

H Automated the filing of quotes.

I **Automated clearing the current screen to enter a new quote.**

J **Designed the printed quote.**

K Added user options to the quotes screen.

L **Customised the interface and added finishing touches.**

M Added the Front End and further options.

Six of the steps are documented in this section to show the student an approach to documentation.

The tasks documented are shown in bold.

Implementation dos

■ Be clear and concise.

■ Use screen dumps to support your explanation.

■ Describe clearly the features of the software you have used.

■ Describe any validation you have included.

Implementation dont's

■ Don't undersell the work you have done and remember exam board moderators can only give credit for what they can see.

■ Don't submit self-generating code and claim it as work done by you!

■ Don't reproduce large tracts of Excel manuals.

A. Setting up the Insurance Groups worksheet with details of cars and insurance groups.

I entered the makes, models and insurance groups of cars in cells A1 to D21 and the insurance group costs into cells H1 to I21. Each make of car has a number attached in column A which will later be used to lookup the car details.

I named the areas A1 to E21 **Groups** and H1 to I21 **Costs** as the **Name** box shows below.

Costs								
Groups		e	Model	IG	CarName	F	G	IG	Basic Cost
2	1	Peugeot	106	3	=B2&" "&C2			1	174
3	2	Peugeot	206	3	=B3&" "&C3			2	180
4	3	Peugeot	306	4	=B4&" "&C4			3	187
5	4	Peugeot	406	10	=B5&" "&C5			4	194
6	5	Peugeot	806	10	=B6&" "&C6			5	202
7	6	Ford	Ka	2	=B7&" "&C7			6	210
8	7	Ford	Fiesta	4	=B8&" "&C8			7	222
9	8	Ford	Escort	5	=B9&" "&C9			8	235
10	9	Ford	Puma	9	=B10&" "&C10			9	248
11	10	Ford	Focus	5	=B11&" "&C11			10	264
12	11	Ford	Mondeo	8	=B12&" "&C12			11	280
13	12	Ford	Galaxy	11	=B13&" "&C13			12	300
14	13	Honda	Civic	9	=B14&" "&C14			13	324
15	14	Honda	Prelude	14	=B15&" "&C15			14	362
16	15	Honda	Accord	8	=B16&" "&C16			15	417
17	16	Reliant	Robin	6	=B17&" "&C17			16	493
18	17	Rover	100	3	=B18&" "&C18			17	600
19	18	Rover	200	6	=B19&" "&C19			18	720
20	19	Rover	400	8	=B20&" "&C20			19	838
21	20	Rover	800	12	=B21&" "&C21			20	945

I want to use a combo box to list the make and model of cars. I needed to add the make to model using the Concatenate function shown in column E. In this way Peugeot in B4 would be added to 306 in C4, giving Peugeot 306 in E4.

C. Setting up the Quotes worksheet with the input controls to enter the driver details.

	A	B	C	D	E
6			Forename		
7			Surname		
8			Address 1		
9			Address 2		
10			Postcode		
11				◉ Male	
12			Sex	○ Female	1
13					
14			Car	Peugeot 306 ▼	3
15					
16			Age	35-39 ▼	5
17					
18			Area	Medium risk ▲	3
19				Low risk ▼	
20			Type	Fully comprehensive ▲	2
21				Third party, fire & theft ▼	

This part of the system deals with the part of the worksheet where the driver options are entered.

The customer's name and address labels were entered into cells C6-C10. Labels for Sex, Car, Age, Area and Type were entered in the cells C12-C20 as shown.

Two option boxes were placed over D11 and D12 linked to cell E12. The number returned in E12 gives the sex of the driver, 1 for male and 2 for female.

I dragged a combo box over cell D14 and linked it to cell E14. I set the input range to Groups!E2:E21. This will allow the drop down to display the cars listed in column E on the Groups worksheet.

In the same way I dragged a combo box over cell D16 and linked it to cell E16. I set the input range to the cells B2:B11 on the Multipliers worksheet. The drop down will display the age ranges for the driver.

List boxes were also set up for Area and Insurance Type linked to the cells shown above. They were designed to pull in the information needed from the Multipliers worksheet.

22			Driver	☑ Extra Driver	TRUE
23				Years	Percent
24			No claims ▲	2	40%
25			▼		
26					

In cell D22 I placed a check box linked to cell E22. It returns TRUE when checked and FALSE when not.

22		Driver	☑ Extra Driver	TRUE
23			Years	Percent
24		No claims ▲		=VLOOKUP(D24,Multipliers!B25:C29,2)
25		▼		

I set a spinner control over cell D24 linked to cell D24, setting the minimum value to 0 and maximum to 4 to allow for up to 4 years no claims discount.

In E24 I used a LOOKUP function to pick up the contents of cell D24 and find the no claims discount from the range of values between B25 and C29 on the Multipliers worksheet.

The numbers returned in column E are used next to establish the details needed for the quote.

■ E. Calculating the total cost of the quote.

The cost of the quote is calculated by multiplying the numbers in column H. The no claims discount is picked up from cell E24.

F	G	H
Make	Peugeot	
Model	406	
IG	10	264
Sex	M	1.3
Age	40-44	1.2
Risk	H	2.4
Extra Driver	Y	1.3
No claims	4	
Type	TP	0.39
Total without discount		£501.13
No claims discount		£300.68
Total cost		£200.45

The formulas were set up as shown below

Total without discount	=H8*H9*H10*H11*H12*H14
No claims discount	=H16*E24
Total cost	=H16-H18

□ I. Clearing the current screen to enter a new quote

After a quote has been made I needed to clear the screen for the next quote.

The areas on the screen that need clearing are cells D6-D10, E12-E22 and cell D24.

I recorded a macro called clearscreen. I highlighted in turn the areas D6-D10 and D24 and clicked Edit, Clear, All. I highlighted cells E12-E22 and clicked Edit, Clear, Contents.

I finished the macro by returning the cursor to D6 ready for the next quote.

A	B	C	D	E
5				
6		Forename	Charles	
7		Surname	George	
8		Address 1	16 Main St	
9		Address 2	Derby	
10		Postcode	DE45 6LU	
11			⦿ Male	
12		Sex	○ Female	1
13				
14		Car	Ford Mondeo ▼	11
15				
16		Age	50-54 ▼	8
17				
18		Area	Medium risk ▲	2
19			Low risk ▼	
20		Type	Fully comprehensive ▲	1
21			Third party, fire & theft ▼	
22		Driver	☑ Extra Driver	TRUE
23			Years	Percent
24		No claims ▲	4	60%
25		▼		

The macro code generated is shown below.

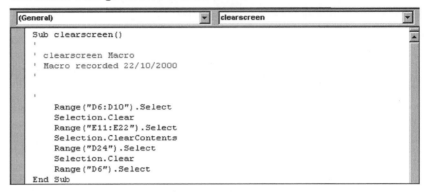

```
(General)                                    clearscreen

  Sub clearscreen()
  '
  ' clearscreen Macro
  ' Macro recorded 22/10/2000
  '

  '
      Range("D6:D10").Select
      Selection.Clear
      Range("E11:E22").Select
      Selection.ClearContents
      Range("D24").Select
      Selection.Clear
      Range("D6").Select
  End Sub
```

J. Designing the printed quote

I have designed the letter to look like this:

P.B Insurance Services

P.B Insurance Services Ltd., Ascot Drive, Derby, DE65 6EX
Tel. (01332) 583939   Fax. (01332) 583911

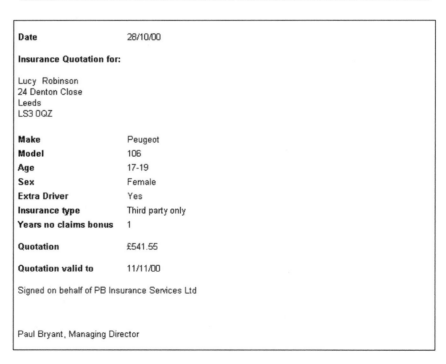

Date	28/10/00
Insurance Quotation for:	
Lucy Robinson	
24 Denton Close	
Leeds	
LS3 0QZ	
Make	Peugeot
Model	106
Age	17-19
Sex	Female
Extra Driver	Yes
Insurance type	Third party only
Years no claims bonus	1
Quotation	£541.55
Quotation valid to	11/11/00

Signed on behalf of PB Insurance Services Ltd

Paul Bryant, Managing Director

▢ L. Customising the interface and added finishing touches

My original interface looked like this:

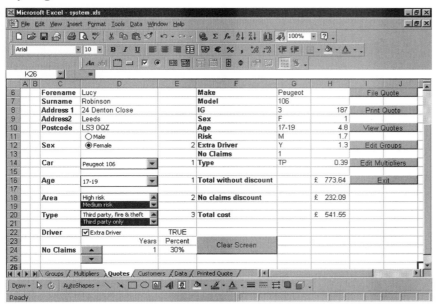

I have customised this interface to look like this using the drawing tools in Excel and the company logo:

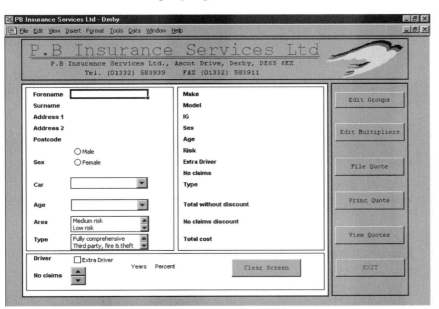

Further development

The implementation section would go on to explain and illustrate how each of the other sub-tasks was implemented.

3. Testing

Results of your tests (following your test plan) should be fully documented including evidence (screen shots). If an outcome is not what was expected, explain why and document what you did to correct the error.

Label all printouts from your system.

Include any user testing and comments.

Examples are shown below.

Test results

■ THE INSURANCE GROUPS WORKSHEET

Test Number	Purpose of Test	Test Data Used	Expected Outcome	Actual Outcome and Comments
1	Test the CONC function in column E combines contents of columns B and C	All makes and models in named range Groups	Make and Model combined with space in between	See Test output 1 No problems, ensure space between speech marks

	A	B	C	D	E	F	G	H	I
1	Number	Make	Model	IG	CarName			IG	Basic Cost
2	1	Peugeot	106	3	Peugeot 106			1	£ 174.00
3	2	Peugeot	206	3	Peugeot 206			2	£ 180.00
4	3	Peugeot	306	4	Peugeot 306			3	£ 187.00
5	4	Peugeot	406	10	Peugeot 406			4	£ 194.00
6	5	Peugeot	806	10	Peugeot 806			5	£ 202.00
7	6	Ford	Ka	2	Ford Ka			6	£ 210.00
8	7	Ford	Fiesta	4	Ford Fiesta			7	£ 222.00
9	8	Ford	Escort	5	Ford Escort			8	£ 235.00
10	9	Ford	Puma	9	Ford Puma			9	£ 248.00
11	10	Ford	Focus	5	Ford Focus			10	£ 264.00
12	11	Ford	Mondeo	8	Ford Mondeo			11	£ 280.00
13	12	Ford	Galaxy	11	Ford Galaxy			12	£ 300.00
14	13	Honda	Civic	9	Honda Civic			13	£ 324.00
15	14	Honda	Prelude	14	Honda Prelude			14	£ 362.00
16	15	Honda	Accord	8	Honda Accord			15	£ 417.00
17	16	Reliant	Robin	6	Reliant Robin			16	£ 493.00
18	17	Rover	100	3	Rover 100			17	£ 600.00
19	18	Rover	200	6	Rover 200			18	£ 720.00
20	19	Rover	400	8	Rover 400			19	£ 838.00
21	20	Rover	800	12	Rover 800			20	£ 945.00
22									
23									
24									
25									

Groups / Sheet2 / Sheet3 /

■ TEST OUTPUT 1

Makes and models in columns B and C combined and results in column E.

■ SETTING UP THE QUOTES WORKSHEET –

Testing the input controls for entering the driver details

Test Number	Purpose of Test	Test Data Used	Expected Outcome	Actual Outcome and Comments
2	Test Option buttons (Sex)	Click on male/female	Returns 1 or 2 in E12	See Test Output 2
3	Test Combo box (Car) returns correct values	Ford Ka	Returns 6 in E14	See Test Output 2
4	Test Combo box (Age) returns correct values	60-65	Returns 10 in E16	See Test Output 2
5	Test Area List box returns correct values	Low risk	Returns 3 in E18	See Test Output 2
6	Test Type List box returns correct values	Fully comprehensive	Returns 1 in E20	See Test Output 2
7	Test Check box returns TRUE/FALSE	Check the check box and uncheck it	Returns TRUE/FALSE in E22	See Test Output 2
8	Test the Spinner control and LOOKUP returns correct discount	Increment spinner to 2 years	40% should be looked up and returned in E24	See Test Output 2 No problems to report on Test 2

■ TEST OUTPUT 2

	A	B	C	D	E
5					
6			Forename		
7			Surname		
8			Address 1		
9			Address 2		
10			Postcode		
11				◉ Male	
12			Sex	○ Female	1
13					
14			Car	Ford Ka ▼	6
15					
16			Age	60-65 ▼	10
17					
18			Area	Medium risk ▲	3
19				Low risk ▼	
20			Type	Fully comprehensive ▲	1
21				Third party, fire & theft ▼	
22			Driver	☑ Extra Driver	TRUE
23				Years	Percent
24			No claims ▲	2	40%
25				▼	

■ CALCULATING THE TOTAL COST OF THE QUOTE

Test Number	Purpose of Test	Test Data Used	Expected Outcome	Actual Outcome and Comments
15	Test the formulas H16, H18 and H20 calculate bill correctly	Peugeot 406, Male, Age 40-44, High Risk, Third Party, Extra driver	Bill worked out on calculator. Total cost = £200.45	See Test output 5 No problems Range of data used

■ TEST OUTPUT 5

The total cost was calculated correctly.

	F	G	H
Make		Peugeot	
Model		406	
IG		10	264
Sex		M	1.3
Age		40-44	1.2
Risk		H	2.4
Extra Driver		Y	1.3
No claims		4	
Type		TP	0.39
Total without discount			£501.13
No claims discount			£300.68
Total cost			£200.45

■ AUTOMATING THE FILING OF QUOTES

Test Number	Purpose of Test	Test Data Used	Expected Outcome	Actual Outcome and Comments
16	Test the macro 'filequote' to see if data is transferred correctly to the Customers worksheet	Routine data, i.e. short name and address plus car details	On running the macro, details should appear in the Customers sheet	Details appear but in bold print. Quote not formatted to currency. See Test Output 6 **Corrective action taken**. See Test Output 7.
	Test the macro 'filequote' when no data is entered	No data entered	A blank row should appear in the customer sheet	Blank row appears but noughts appear in some cells. See Test Output 8 **Corrective action taken**.

■ TEST OUTPUT 6

	A	B	C	D	E	F	G	H	I	J	K	L	M	N	O
1	Forename	Surname	Address1	Address2	Postcode	Make	Model	IG	Sex	Age	Risk	Extra	NCB	Type	Quote
2	**David**	**Evans**	**94 Belgrave Roa**	**Derby**	**DE2 9TW**	**Ford**	**Escort**	**5**	**M**	**45-49**	**M**	**Y**	**4**	**FC**	**266.96**
3	Harriet	Chalmers	6 The Drive	Cardiff	CF5 9QA	Ford	Ka	2	F	40-44	M	N	2	FC	220.32
4	Bill	Biggins	17 Yarmouth Drive	Tadcaster	YO9 7UH	Peugeot		806	10	M	50-54	L	N	4	FC	151.01
5	Dave	Hunt	12 South St	Derby	DE4 4RF	Peugeot		206	3	M	20-24	L	Y	2	FC	455.08
6	Peter	Williams	97 Arthur St	Derby	DE65 6RT	Ford	Fiesta	4	M	45-49	M	Y	3	FC	£320.48
7	Horace	Bachelor	13 Main St	Derby	DE22 3RT	Ford	Ka	2	M	45-49	L	Y	4	FC	£139.93

New record in bold print. Quote not in currency format. The macro was rerecorded, turning off bold. Column O was formatted to currency. The macro was then tested again.

■ TEST OUTPUT 7

New record not in bold print. Quote in currency format.

	A	B	C	D	E	F	G	H	I	J	K	L	M	N	O
1	Forename	Surname	Address1	Address2	Postcode	Make	Model	IG	Sex	Age	Risk	Extra	NCB	Type	Quote
2	Fiona	Allder	76 The Walks	Markeaton	DE4 8HB	Peugeot		306	4	F	25-29	M	N	3	FC	£329.80
3	David	Evans	94 Belgrave Road	Derby	DE2 9TW	Ford	Escort		5	M	45-49	M	Y	4	FC	£266.96
4	Harriet	Chalmers	6 The Drive	Cardiff	CF5 9QA	Ford	Ka		2	F	40-44	M	N	2	FC	£220.32
5	Bill	Biggins	17 Yarmouth Drive	Tadcaster	YO9 7UH	Peugeot		806	10	M	50-54	L	N	4	FC	£151.01
6	Dave	Hunt	12 South St	Derby	DE4 4RF	Peugeot		206	3	M	20-24	L	Y	2	FC	£455.08
7	Peter	Williams	97 Arthur St	Derby	DE65 6RT	Ford	Fiesta		4	M	45-49	M	Y	3	FC	£320.48
8	Horace	Bachelor	13 Main St	Derby	DE22 3RT	Ford	Ka		2	M	45-49	L	Y	4	FC	£139.93

■ TEST OUTPUT 8

Extra row appears. Noughts appear in cells A2 to E2. Corrective action was taken to put instructions in the user guide on how to remove unwanted rows.

	A	B	C	D	E	F	G	H	I	J	K	L	M	N	O
1	Forename	Surname	Address1	Address2	Postcode	Make	Model	IG	Sex	Age	Risk	Extra	NCB	Type	Quote
2	0	0	0	0	0										
3	Fiona	Allder	76 The Walks	Markeaton	DE4 8HB	Peugeot		306	4	F	25-29	M	N	3	FC	£329.80
4	David	Evans	94 Belgrave Road	Derby	DE2 9TW	Ford	Escort		5	M	45-49	M	Y	4	FC	£266.96
5	Harriet	Chalmers	6 The Drive	Cardiff	CF5 9QA	Ford	Ka		2	F	40-44	M	N	2	FC	£220.32
6	Bill	Biggins	17 Yarmouth Drive	Tadcaster	YO9 7UH	Peugeot		806	10	M	50-54	L	N	4	FC	£151.01
7	Dave	Hunt	12 South St	Derby	DE4 4RF	Peugeot		206	3	M	20-24	L	Y	2	FC	£455.08
8	Peter	Williams	97 Arthur St	Derby	DE65 6RT	Ford	Fiesta		4	M	45-49	M	Y	3	FC	£320.48
9	Horace	Bachelor	13 Main St	Derby	DE22 3RT	Ford	Ka		2	M	45-49	L	Y	4	FC	£139.93

■ ADDING THE FRONT END AND FURTHER OPTIONS

Test Number	Purpose of Test	Test Data Used	Expected Outcome	Actual Outcome and Comments
26	Test again the auto_open macro	Start the system up	System loads Front End screen	Front end loads when file is opened. See Test Output 9.

■ TEST OUTPUT 9

Front end loads as expected.

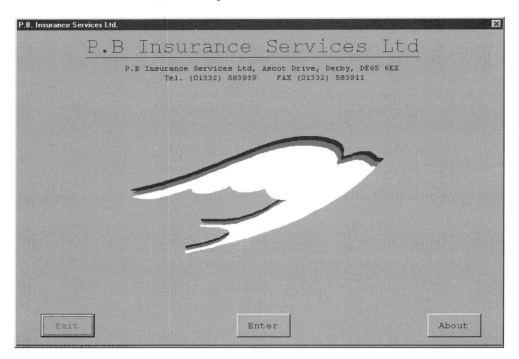

□ (b) User testing

After Paul had used the system for a few days he made the following observations.

- The system issued quotes easily and quickly which was particularly useful when dealing with phone enquiries.

- Paul would have liked the system to produce carbon copies of the quote automatically as opposed to clicking Print a number of times.

- He thought the system was potentially user friendly but he certainly had reservations about the Start up screen. All he wanted to do was get started and that slowed him down and eventually became irritating during the course of the day.

- When entering details of the customer he wasn't sure how much space he had to enter the name and address in. He thought the printed quote would have had more of a professional feel if it had had a footer as well as the header.

He liked the interface as did his assistant but he found the look and feel of other screen options, e.g. the Customers, Groups completely different, far more like Excel. This was a little off-putting.

As he used the system the file of customer quotes built up very quickly, eventually going off the screen. He found he needed advice as to how to search for a particular quote.

Both Paul and his assistant were worried about how to back up the system and transfer files to the laptop for out of hours use.

User guide

A user guide is just that – a guide for the **user** or **users** of your system.

It should include details of:

- the purpose of the system;

- the minimum system requirements needed to run your system, e.g. Pentium 200 with 64Mb of memory;

- how to get started;

- the main menu options;

- how to perform each of the routine tasks that make up your system;

- common problems or error messages and possible solutions;

- security measures, backup procedures and passwords needed.

4. User Guide to the Car Insurance Quotation system

Introduction

The system allows the user to issue car insurance quotes both on screen and to printer. It enables the user to file away quotes and store for later reference in a user friendly manner.

System requirements

You require a minimum of a Pentium PC with 64Mb of memory. Microsoft Office 2000 needs to be installed including the component Excel 2000. The system uses initially 137Kb of disc space and hence the size of hard drive is not important. A laser printer is recommended to ensure fast, high quality output.

How to install the system

The system is supplied on a 1.44Mb floppy disc. It is recommended that the file is installed to your hard drive.

1. On the Desktop create a New Folder by right clicking the mouse button. Name the folder PB Insurance.

2. Insert the floppy disc containing the system.

3. Click on the My Computer icon and then the Floppy drive A icon.

4. Drag the file called Derby on to the folder PB Insurance.

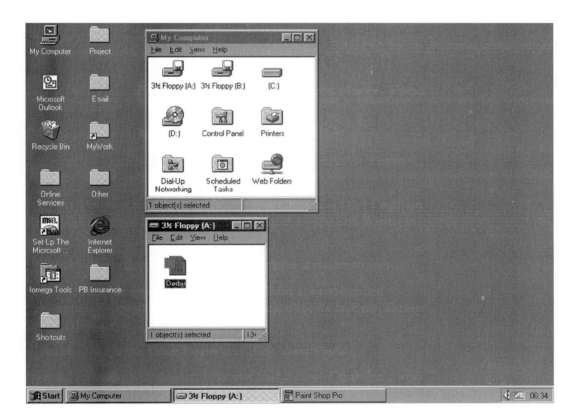

Getting started

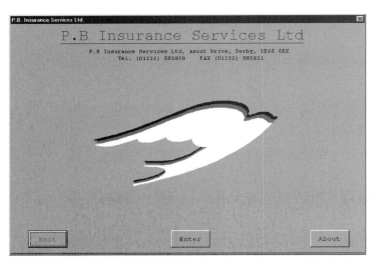

To boot up the system double click the file icon called Derby.

The system displays its **Start Up** screen with details of the company PB Insurance.

The user is presented with three options.

1. Clicking the **Exit** button closes the system down.

2. Clicking the **Enter** button enters the system.

3. Clicking the **About** button offers further information about the system.

The user options

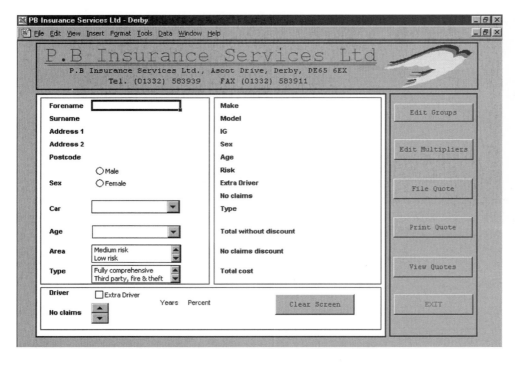

To enter the system click the **Enter** button on the **Start Up** screen.

From this screen the user has access to a number of options by simply clicking the button.

Issue a quote by entering the driver details.

✈ **Edit Groups** allows the user to change the cars and insurance ratings.

✈ **Edit Multipliers** allows the user to edit the multiplying factors.

✈ **File Quote** stores the quote in the system for later reference.

✈ **Print Quote** outputs a copy of the quote to the printer.

✈ **View Quotes** allows the user to view previously stored quotes.

✈ **Clear Screen** removes the current quote from screen ready for a new entry.

✈ **Exit** closes down the system.

How to issue a quote

Once the system has loaded clicking enter on the **Start Up** screen brings the user to the **Quotes** screen.

It is automatically ready to issue a quote with the cursor at Forename of driver.

If a quote is currently on screen then click the **Clear Screen** option.

Enter the name and address of the customer in the appropriate cells as shown below.

The driver and car details are easily entered by clicking the drop downs and clicking your choice.

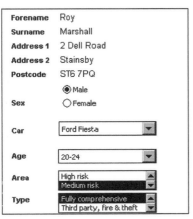

An extra driver can be added by checking the extra driver check box below.

The driver's no claims discount can easily be entered by increasing or decreasing the spinner control.

When the details are complete click the **Print Quote** option for a printed quote. Click the **File Quote** option to store the quote for later reference.

Further development

It is likely that the user guide for this system would go on to include:

Details of the other user options such as:

➤ how to edit details of the cars available by using the edit groups option;

➤ how to edit details of the multiplying factors;

➤ instructions for filing, viewing and printing quotes.

Possible problems and troubleshooting.

Instructions for backing up the system during daily operation – both when and how.

Also consideration would be given to copying the system between PC and laptop when the user needs to work away from the office.

User guide do's

■ It should contain simple, clear, step by step instructions to using your system.

■ It should be jargon free and well illustrated.

■ It might form or be part of online help built into the system.

User guide dont's

■ It should not be a guide to using the software but a guide to your system.

■ Don't include large tracts of text from user manuals and try to avoid using jargon.

Evaluation

This section requires the student to report on their project.

5. Evaluation report

To evaluate my system I will look at the initial end user requirements and also take on board comments made by the users when testing the system.

1. **A system is required to be able to give a quick quote accurately and efficiently**.

   The system produced does issue quotes accurately. The system was tested thoroughly and no errors found during the trial period with Paul Bryant. It enabled both users to deal with on line phone enquiries far more quickly.

2. **The system must produce multiple copies of the quote**.

   At present you have to repeat the print process for however many quotes you wish to issue. I will look at automating this in the future to issue a carbon copy of the quote.

3. **The system should enable phone enquiries to be dealt with far more quickly than at present**.

   A test comparison was held between the old manual system and the new system. The old system took 2 minutes 14 seconds. The new system took 32 seconds to enter the details and file the quote.

4. **Issued quotes need to be stored with the facility to view at a later date**.

   Quotes can be stored effectively but real improvements need to be made here. The database will build up very quickly and the user will need experience of Excel to be able to search and retrieve information about the quotes filed away. I need to add instructions to the User Guide on how to tackle this.

5. **Quotes should be issued with a professional look on letter-headed paper**.

   The quote itself was felt to be professionally produced but future versions will come with a footer.

6. **The system must be user friendly, yet have a professional look and feel**.

The user feels the system is user-friendly but when entering customer details it is not clear how many characters are allowed for each item of data. I may investigate the use of validation checks here or simply advise the user in the user guide.

The other user screens need customising along the lines of the quotes screen to be consistent and give a common feel to the system.

7. **The system should be able to be transferred easily between the laptop and office-based PC**.

The initial system uses 137Kb of disc space. Using copy and paste I added 1000 customers, which increased the file size to 375Kb. The system can be easily transferred using a floppy disk.

Limitations and possible enhancements

I might in a future version of the system remove the start up screen by adjusting the auto_open macro so that start up is quicker for the users.

I could customise the user interface further by running the whole system from a User Form.

It might be easier to handle if every quote was issued with a quote reference number and a date of issue to aid searching in the future.

Over a period of time this file will get very large and the user needs to establish procedures for clearing out quotes that are not needed or are past renewal. This could be manually done in Excel but I might try to automate this feature in the future.

Both users were worried and concerned about backups and transfer of files between laptop and PC. A system needs to be implemented such that a backup is made whenever a quote is issued and procedures in place so that quotes are never issued on more than one machine. I will provide advice in the User Guide.

It is unlikely disc space will be a problem but a Zip drive may provide greater security.

Evaluation do's

■ You should look at original your end user requirements and report on whether you have achieved what you wanted to including successes, problems and possible solutions.

■ No system is perfect. There will always be room for improvement. Outline any limitations and possible further developments

Evaluation don'ts

■ Don't moan about the lack of time. Time management is your responsibility.

■ Don't pretend it is all working when some parts are incomplete. Do not be afraid to tell the truth.

■ Don't report on how well you did but focus on how well your system achieved its aims.

Presenting coursework to hand in

When your project is finished you should:

➤ Produce a front cover. Your name, centre and candidate number should be clear.

➤ Get your project in order. Page numbering and the use of headers and footers are to be encouraged.

➤ Produce a contents page which clearly cross references to each section in the project.

➤ Bind your project securely. Often coursework has to be sent for checking. It needs to be firmly attached but ring binders are not encouraged.

50 Excel tricks and tips

Here are fifty tricks and tips that have been found to be more than useful in implementing Excel projects. Many of them have been discovered by students themselves.

1. Getting more than one line of text in a cell
2. A quick way of displaying formulas
3. Putting a tick into a cell
4. Making an entry fit the cell
5. Linking a text box to data in a cell
6. Formatting non-adjacent areas
7. Using the Drag Copy short cut
8. Using AutoFill to enter data quickly
9. What is a circular reference?
10. What is the difference between Paste and Paste Link?
11. Inserting multiple rows and columns
12. Quickly copying cell formats to other cells or cell ranges
13. Using angled text to improve your presentation
14. Switching rows of cells to columns or columns to rows
15. Putting the title across many cells (merge and centre)
16. Displaying the date and time
17. Entering the current Date or Time quickly
18. Fixing problems with dates
19. Entering numbers as text
20. Calculating with dates
21. What day of the week is a date?
22. Hiding columns
23. Hiding the contents of a cell
24. Improving the format of a table. (AutoFormat)
25. Setting how your worksheets will look at the start (Format Style)
26. Creating an automatic backup of your work
27. A quick way of closing all those open files

■ 1. Getting more than one line of text in a cell

Press ALT+ENTER to start a new line in the same cell.

Or if your text is too long to fit in a cell, highlight the cells, and click on **Format, Cells.**

Click on the **Alignment** tab and click on **Wrap text**. The text will be displayed on multiple lines.

The total number voting in favour was 31

2. A quick way of displaying formulas

	A	B	C
1	1	2	=A1*B1
2	3	6	=A2*B2
3	6	5	=A3*B3
4	4	6	=A4*B4
5			=SUM(C1:C4)

Hold down the CTRL + ` (next to 1 on the keyboard). This will switch to showing formulas. Press these keys again to return to normal mode.

3. Putting a tick into a cell

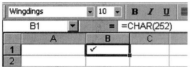

Enter in the cell =CHAR(252) and set the font to **Wingdings** font.

You can now copy this to other cells.

4. Making an entry fit the cell

Excel can automatically resize the text to fit into a cell if you don't want the cell to shrink or grow to accommodate an entry.

Highlight the cell(s), click on **Format, Cells, Alignment** and check the **Shrink To Fit** box.

	A	B	C	D
1	Company	Number he	Purchase price	

Before

	A	B	C
1	Company	Number held	Purchase price

After

5. Linking a text box to data in a cell

You can link a text box so that it displays the contents of a cell. To do this, follow these steps:

Click on the **Text Box** icon on the **Drawing** toolbar, click and drag out a text box on the worksheet.

Click in the formula bar and enter = followed by the cell location e.g. =A7 if you want the contents of A7 to be displayed in the text box.

■ 6. Formatting non-adjacent areas

If you want to format groups of cells on a worksheet that are not next to each other, you need to select them. Do this by:

1. dragging to select the first group of cells;

2. holding CTRL down and dragging across any other groups of cells.

Use this method if you want to draw a graph of data in non-adjacent cells.

■ 7. Using the Drag Copy short cut

When a cell is selected there is a small black square in the bottom right hand corner. If you move the cursor over this square, it changes from the usual white cross to a hairline black cross.

If you now drag this cross down to other cells it will copy the contents of first cell to all the others, it will also make an intelligent guess at a sequence.

Try the operation on a word, a formula, Product 1, a day, a month in a cell.

	A	B	C	D	E	F
1						
2		Good	=F5*E5	Product 1	Monday	January
3		Good	=F6*E6	Product 2	Tuesday	February
4		Good	=F7*E7	Product 3	Wednesday	March
5		Good	=F8*E8	Product 4	Thursday	April
6		Good	=F9*E9	Product 5	Friday	May

If you enter the first two numbers of a number sequence or a date sequence, highlight both cells and drag down, the sequence continues:

	A	B	C	D
1				
2		2		7-Jan
3		4		14-Jan
4		6		21-Jan
5		8		28-Jan
6		10		4-Feb

8. Using AutoFill to enter data quickly

Another way of performing the same operation is to:

1. enter the first piece of data in the series;

2. highlight the cells you wish to fill;

3. click on **Edit, Fill, Series**;

4. click on **AutoFill,** enter the **Step value** and then click on **OK**.

9. What is a circular reference?

Type = A6 + A7 into A7.

You will see this error message.

This is because the formula in A7 refers to A7. This error is called a circular reference.

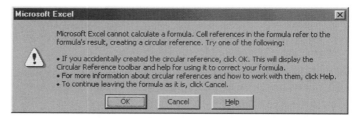

10. What is the difference between Paste and Paste Link?

When you copy data from one cell and paste it into another cell, if the first cell changes the second cell does not change.

By using **Paste Link** you can link the two cells, so that if the first cell is updated, so is the second.

1. Click on the source cell and click on the **Copy** icon.

2. Click on the second cell and click on **Edit, Paste Special.**

3. Click on the **Paste Link** button.

■ 11. Inserting multiple rows and columns

If you need to insert one row, select a row by clicking on the row number, right click and click on **Insert**.

To insert multiples (for example three rows), select three rows, right click and click on **Insert**. Three rows will be inserted. This also works for columns.

■ 12. Quickly copying cell formats to other cells or cell ranges

1. Click on the cell whose formatting you wish to copy.

2. Click on **Format Painter** icon (a paintbrush picture on the **Formatting** toolbar).

3. Click on the cell or cell range you want to copy the formatting to.

> **Note**
> ■ To continue formatting to a number of locations double click Format Painter and click the button again when you have finished.

■ 13. Using angled text to improve your Presentation

To put text at an angle:

1. Highlight the cells B2:B7 and click on **Format, Cells.**

2. Click on the **Alignment** tab.

3. Enter the required angle or drag this guide-line around the 'clock face.'

> **Note**
> ■ Angled text loses its sharpness.

	A	B	C
1			
2		Price	£10,000.00
3		Deposit	£5,000.00
4		Loan	£5,000.00
5		Rate	10%
6		Years	3
7		Payment	-£161.34

Orientation: 90 Degrees

	A	B	C
1			
2		Price	£10,000.00
3		Deposit	£5,000.00
4		Loan	£5,000.00
5		Rate	10%
6		Years	3
7		Payment	-£161.34

14. Switching rows of cells to columns or columns to rows

How can we change this:

	A	B	C	D
1	1	Powell	Jackie	Mrs
2	2	Baker	John	Mr
3	3	Green	Dennis	Mr
4	4	Blocker	Kath	Mrs
5	5	Jones	Angela	Mrs
6	6	Mahmood	Kashif	Mr
7	7	Jones	Heather	Miss
8	8	Brown	Bill	Mr

into this?

	A	B	C	D	E	F	G	H
1	1	2	3	4	5	6	7	8
2	Powell	Baker	Green	Blocker	Jones	Mahmood	Jones	Brown
3	Jackie	John	Dennis	Kath	Angela	Kashif	Heather	Bill
4	Mrs	Mr	Mr	Mrs	Mrs	Mr	Miss	Mr

1. Select the cells that you want to switch.

2. Click on **Edit, Copy**.

3. Click on the top-left cell of the paste area. The paste area must be outside the copy area. In the above example, a new worksheet has been used.

4. Click on **Edit, Paste Special**.

5. Select the **Transpose** check box. Click on **OK**.

15. Putting the title across many cells (Merge and Center)

To centre a heading across a range of cells e.g. A1 to G1:

1. Enter the heading into cell A1.

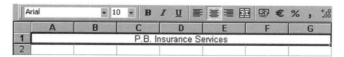

Arial		10		B	I	U						€	%	,	

	A	B	C	D	E	F	G
1			P.B. Insurance Services				
2							

2. Highlight the cells A1 to G1.

3. Click on the **Merge and Center** icon.

To remove Merge and Center, click on the **Format Painter** icon and then click on the last merged cell.

◾ 16. Displaying the date and time

To enter the date and time into an Excel worksheet:

1. Click on the required cell.

2. Enter `=TODAY()` for today's date.

3. Enter `=NOW()` for today's date and the current time.

    The format may not be exactly how you require the date.

4. Use **Format, Cells** to format the date or time as required using the options shown below.

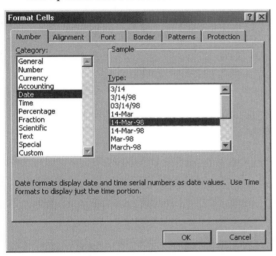

Dates and times entered using =TODAY() or =NOW() will be updated when you next open the file.

◾ 17. Entering the current date or time quickly

To enter the current date in a cell, press CTRL and **;** (semi-colon)

To enter the current time in a cell, press CTRL and **:** (colon)

Dates and times entered using this method will **NOT** be updated when you next open the file.

18. Fixing problems with dates

Sometimes the date appears as a number like 36680. This is because Excel stores dates as numbers in order starting on 1 January 1900 which is stored as 1.

For example, 3 June 2000 is stored as 36680. To change the number back to a date, click on **Format, Cells** and select **Date**.

19. Entering numbers as text

If you wish to enter a number as a code e.g. 000262, Excel will store it as a number and only display 262.

To enter 000262, type in an apostrophe first **'000262**. The apostrophe formats the cell to text format. 000262 is displayed and not the apostrophe.

However the apostrophe is displayed in the formula bar.

Similarly, you might have conducted a survey and typed 1-4, 5-8 and 9-12 into three cells. Excel changes them to 1 April, 5 August and 9 December.

This is because Excel has formatted the cells as dates. To prevent this, type an apostrophe at the start of the data, e.g. '1-4.

20. Calculating with dates

Use the DATEDIF function to calculate the number of days, months or years between dates, for example, to work out how old someone is or for how many days a book has been borrowed.

1. Put the first date in A1.

2. Type `=NOW()` in A2.

3. Type `=DATEDIF(A1,A2,"y")` in A3.

You will see the difference between the two dates in full years.

Use **"m"** for the number of full months in the period and **"d"** for the number of days.

■ 21. What day of the week is a date?

1. Type a date in A1

2. Type `=WEEKDAY(A1)` in A2

1 means Sunday, 2 means Monday and so on.

■ 22. Hiding columns

Suppose you want to hide all of column C from the user.

1. Select column C by clicking on the C in the column heading at the top.

2. Right click anywhere on the column.

3. Click on **Hide**.

To remove this feature:

1. Highlight the two columns on either side of the hidden column. (B and D).

2. Right click anywhere on one of these columns.

3. Click on **Unhide**.

■ 23. Hiding the contents of a cell

1. Select the cell(s) you wish to hide

2. Click on **Format, Cells** and the click on the **Number** tab.

3. In the **Category** list click on **Custom**

4. In the **Type** box select the existing codes and delete

5. In the **Type** box enter **;;;** (three semicolons)

> **Note**
> ■ to undo this click on **Format, Cells, Number**. In the **Category** list click on whatever category the cell was before, e.g. General, Number, Currency, Date, etc.

■ 24. Improving the format of a table (AutoFormat)

1. Click on any cell in a table of data

2. Click on **Format, AutoFormat** to format the table.

You will be given a choice of several different formats that you may wish to use.

Use this function to make your tables look smarter.

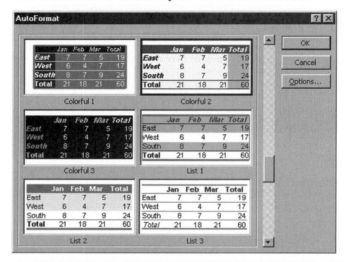

■ 25. Setting how your worksheets will look at the start (Format Style)

If you want all your worksheets to be in a different font or colour:

1. Click on **Format, Style**.

2. The box below appears. Click on **Modify** to change the general format of cells, such as colour of background, borders, fonts, etc.

The style will change for all worksheets in the workbook.

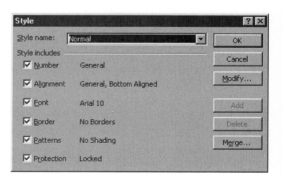

26. Creating an automatic backup of your work

Excel allows you to create an automatic backup of a file as you work, so that you cannot lose all your work if the system crashes.

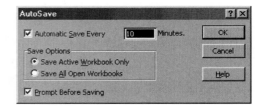

1. Click on **Tools, AutoSave**.

2. Check the box and set the file to be saved every 5 minutes.

> **Note**
>
> ■ AutoSave is an Add-In which is not automatically installed with Excel.

If AutoSave isn't on the Tools menu.

1. Click on **Tools, Add-Ins**

2. Check the **AutoSave Add-In** box.

27. A quick way of closing all those open files

Clicking on **File, Close** only closes the active Excel file.

Close all open Excel files by holding down the SHIFT key and clicking on **File**. **Close All** is now on the menu.

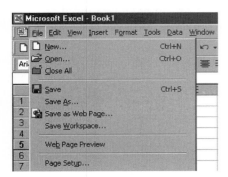

■ 28. Changing the default folder for Excel to store files

1. Click on **Tools, Options** and click on the **General** tab.

2. Enter the path name of the folder you wish to use in the **Default file location**.

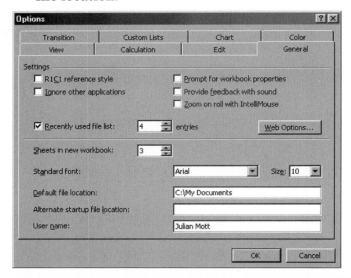

■ 29. Increasing the number of recently used files in the File drop down menu

1. Click on **Tools, Options** and click on the **General** tab as above.

2. In the **Recently used file list** section, enter the required number of files that you wish to see displayed at the bottom of the file drop down menu.

■ 30. Adding comments to your work

A comment is a small on-screen 'Post-It' note that you can attach to a cell to tell the user some more information.

If a cell has a comment attached, there is a red triangle in the top right hand corner of the cell.

As you move the cursor over the cell, the comment appears.

To enter a comment.

1. Click on the cell.

2. Click on **Insert, Comment**

3. Enter the comment.

To delete a comment, right click on the cell and click on **Delete Comment.**

	A	B	C	D	E
1	School Play Ticket Sales				
2	Day	Time			Total
3	Wednesday	evening	First night. Tickets £2.50 child £3.50 adult	76	121
4	Thursday	evening		81	135
5	Friday	evening		120	172
6	Saturday	matinee	92	46	138
7	Saturday	evening	66	106	172

■ 31. Automatically correcting common typing errors (AutoCorrect)

Microsoft Excel has a useful feature called AutoCorrect. Common spelling mistakes are automatically corrected as you type. For example *recieve* would automatically be corrected to *receive*. The word *I* is automatically capitalised.

You can customise it to add your own words using **Tools, AutoCorrect**.

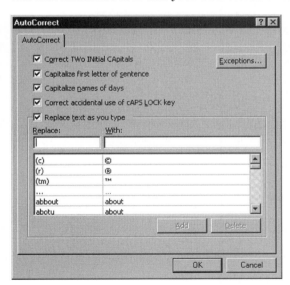

Enter the incorrect word and the correct word into the boxes.

Another useful feature of AutoCorrect is that if you accidentally leave the Caps Lock turned on and type in a name like *sMITH*, it automatically changes the word to *Smith* and turns off the Caps Lock.

The AutoCorrect feature also exists in Microsoft Word.

■ 32. Switching case

If you want to turn the text in a cell to all upper case (capital letters) you can use the UPPER function. e.g. `=UPPER(D2)` will display the text from D2 in upper case

There are similar functions called LOWER and PROPER.

LOWER e.g. `=LOWER(D2)` turns text into lower case (small letters).

PROPER e.g. `=PROPER(D2)` turns all words into proper noun form. (The first letter is in upper case and the rest in lower case.)

■ 33. Customising your screen output

You can customise your screen output by clicking on **Tools, Options** and clicking on the **View** tab.

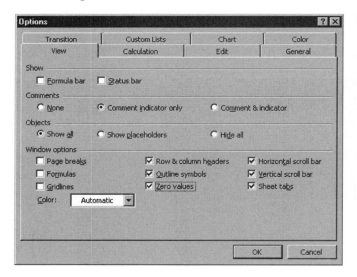

Amongst the options available are:

- zero suppression – leaving a cell blank if its value is zero;

- gridline suppression – hiding the gridlines;

- removing the tabs and scroll bar;

- removing the status bar and the formula bar;

- showing the comment all the time, only when the mouse moves over that cell or not showing it at all.

34. Stopping a header row disappearing off the screen (Freeze panes)

A company has details of customers stored in an Excel worksheet. As they scroll down the page the top line (the heading row) disappears.

	A	B	C	D	E	F	G
8	7	Jones	Heather	Miss	26 Greatley Rd	Tutbury	DE13 3W!
9	8	Brown	Bill	Mr	19 Primrose View	Burton upon Trent	DE14 6RL
10	9	Sands	Eileen	Ms	67 Frindle St	Burton upon Trent	DE14 6TG
11	10	Bird	Elizabeth	Miss	12 The Sands	Matlock	DE35 6YX
12	11	Bryant	Charles	Mr	16 Wardlow Crescent	Derby	DE4 6QA

They want to keep the column headings on the screen. They can do this using **Freeze Panes.**

1. Click on row header 2 to highlight row 2.

2. Click on **Window, Freeze Panes**.

The top line is now locked.

	A	B	C	D	E	F	G
1	Customer	Surname	First name	Title	Street	Area	Postcode
8	7	Jones	Heather	Miss	26 Greatley Rd	Tutbury	DE13 3W
9	8	Brown	Bill	Mr	19 Primrose View	Burton upon Trent	DE14 6RL
10	9	Sands	Eileen	Ms	67 Frindle St	Burton upon Trent	DE14 6TC
11	10	Bird	Elizabeth	Miss	12 The Sands	Matlock	DE35 6Y)
12	11	Bryant	Charles	Mr	16 Wardlow Crescent	Derby	DE4 6QA

3. Test it works.

To turn it off click on **Window, Unfreeze Panes**

35. Linking to the Internet from Excel

You can include hyperlinks (links to Internet pages and email addresses) in Excel.

Clicking on a web page link will load your Internet browser and go to the chosen address.

Clicking on an email address will load your email software so that you can type a message.

To enter a hyperlink:

1. Click on **Insert Hyperlink.**

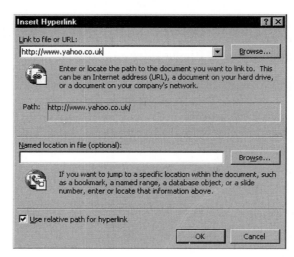

2. Type the Internet address into the top box.

When you click on OK the link will be inserted into your spreadsheet. When you move the mouse over the link. The familiar hand appears to show it is a link.

If you prefer to put the name of the site rather than the address:

1. Type in the site name.

2. Click on **Insert, Hyperlink**.

3. Enter the address as before.

You can choose which you prefer:

It is also possible to put in a hyperlink to another location in your file, for example to another worksheet. Click on the bottom **Browse** button to get this dialogue box.

You can choose the sheet and the cell you wish to link to.

■ 36. Combining the contents of two columns

When storing details of customers' names, it is usual to store the data in three different fields: surname, first name and title:

	A	B	C	D
1	Customer code	Surname	First name	Title
2	1	Powell	Jackie	Mrs
3	2	Baker	John	Mr
4	3	Green	Dennis	Mr
5	4	Blocker	Kath	Mrs
6	5	Jones	Angela	Mrs
7	6	Mahmood	Kashif	Mr
8	7	Jones	Heather	Miss
9	8	Brown	Bill	Mr

This means that we can sort into alphabetical order but can also send out personalised letters. The name on the invoice will be either Mrs Jackie Powell or Mrs J. Powell.

Joining two or more words together into one word is called **CONCATENATION**.

To do this in Excel use the CONCATENATE function using the ampersand key (&) as follows:

1. Enter the above data.

2. In E1 enter the function = D1&C1&B1

3. Copy and paste the function down the column.

	A	B	C	D	E
1	1	Powell	Jackie	Mrs	MrsJackiePowell
2	2	Baker	John	Mr	MrJohnBaker
3	3	Green	Dennis	Mr	MrDennisGreen
4	4	Blocker	Kath	Mrs	MrsKathBlocker

The function joins the text together. You then need to force spaces between the words.

4. In E1 change the function to = D1&" "&C1&" "&B1 (There is a space between the quotation marks.)

5. Copy and paste the function down the column.

If we want the name Mrs J. Powell to appear on the invoice, we need to use the LEFT function.

Mrs J. Powell

=LEFT(C1,1)

This is the first letter of the word in C1.

Join the two functions together as follows:
 = D1&" "&LEFT(C1,1)&" "&B1

Note: There are **RIGHT** and **MID** functions as well.

For example:

RIGHT(D5,3) will take the three characters at the end of the word(s) in D5.

MID(E40, 5, 8) will take 8 characters from the middle of the text in E40, starting at the 5th character.

■ 37. A table stores names as John Smith. How do I split this into John and Smith?

1   Highlight the cells and click on **Data, Text to columns...**

2. A wizard will start. Click in **Delimited** and click on **Next**

3   Check the **Space** box as shown.

4. Click on **Finish**

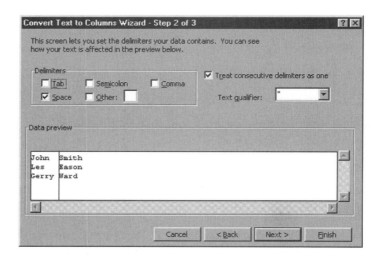

■ 38. Password protecting your files

It is easy to add a password to an Excel file to prevent unauthorised access. When you save your file, click on **File, Save As...**

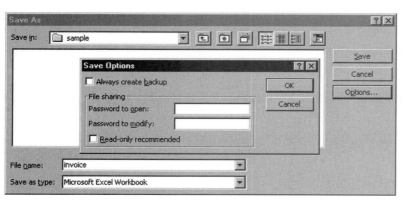

Then click on **Options**. If you wish to add a password, type it in the top box.

You will be asked to re-type the password as verification.

Every time you load this file, you will be asked for the password.

39. What if I forget my password?

In a word, don't.

But if you have, remember that passwords are case sensitive so check that caps lock is turned off.

If this doesn't work, there are companies that produce software to recover such files. You can download them from the Internet. They are **not** free. Try sites like http://www.lostpassword.com/

This just proves that Excel passwords aren't as secure as you might expect.

40. Using help

Online help is available by pressing F1. Type in the keyword and search for advice.

Excel 2000 also has an 'Answer wizard' which enables you to type in a question and get help.

There is a separate but similar online help for Visual Basic.

41. Removing the Office Assistant

The Office Assistant is an on-screen animation that is supposed to be helpful. Many people find it annoying when it suddenly appears without any apparent reason.

To turn off the Office Assistant when it appears:

1. Right click on the Office Assistant .

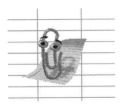

2. Click on **Options**.

3. Uncheck **Use the Office Assistant**.

42. Turning on and off 'Intelligent' menus

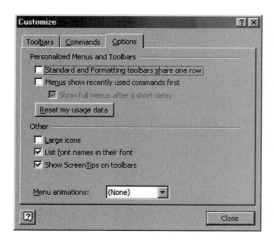

Excel 2000 has an 'intelligent' menu system that displays only the most recent choices. This than be quite annoying as the positions of items on the menus are constantly changing.

To turn off the 'intelligent' menus, click on **Tools, Customize.** Click on the **Options** tab. Uncheck the box for **Menus show recently used commands first**.

Recheck this box to turn the intelligent menu back on.

43. Using Auditing Tools for debugging (Trace)

The **Trace** command helps you with debugging as it tells you which cells will change when you change another cell. These cells are **dependent** on the first cell.

1.   Click on a cell.

2.   Click on **Tools, Auditing, Trace Dependents**.

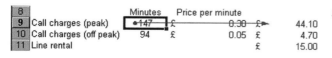

3.   A blue arrow appears pointing to the dependent cell(s). You can repeat the process for this cell to see if it too has any dependents.

Changing the 147 will change the amount in the cell two columns to its right.

Click on **Tools, Auditing, Trace Precedents** to find any cells that affect a cell containing a formula.

Remove the arrows with **Tools, Auditing, Remove All Arrows**.

■ 44. A quick way of entering the name of a range of cells (Paste name)

If you are using a named range of cells in a function such as SUM or VLOOKUP, you do not need to type in the name. Just press F3 to get a list of names available.

■ 45. Using Go To Special

You can use Go To, Special to highlight special cells on your workbook, e.g. cells with formulas, cells with validation, cells with comments or cells with conditional formatting.

1. Click on **Edit, Go To**.

2. Click on the **Special** button.

3. Select the type of cell required.

■ 46. Highlighting changed cells

Click on **Tools, Track Changes, Highlight Changes** and check **Track changes while editing.**

Cells that are changed have a blue triangle in the top left hand corner.

You can choose whether to accept or reject these changes by clicking on **Tools, Track Changes, Accept or Reject Changes**.

■ 47. Splitting panes

Click on **Window, Split** to split your window into four sections. You can scroll on each section separately.

This is very useful if you want to work on two or more parts of the same worksheet that are not close to each other.

Click on **Window, Remove Split** to return to the conventional screen.

■ 48. What is a workspace?

You can group two or more workbooks together by saving them as a workspace file.

A workspace file (***.xlw**) saves details of all open workbooks and their locations, window sizes, and screen positions in one file. To save a workspace:

1. Open all the workbooks you want to group together.

2. Position the workbook windows as you want them to appear when you open them.

3. Click on the **File, Save Workspace**.

> **Note**
>
> ■ The workspace file is a very small file as it only saves details about the stored workbooks and not the contents of the workbooks themselves.

■ 49. Useful Web sites

There are many Internet sites offering tips and hints in using Excel. As with all Internet sites, the quality varies, good sites can be hard to find and sites are appearing and disappearing all the time.

Go to any search engine and search on *Excel Hints*. Here are just a few examples:

1. http://www.microsoft.com/office/ is full of information tips, tricks, and how-to articles and frequently asked questions for Microsoft Office programs like Excel.

2. http://support.microsoft.com/ has a knowledge base search to search for technical support information and self-help tools for Microsoft products.

3. http://www.pcworld.com/heres_how/category/0,1696,Spreadsheet, 00.html has lots of good spreadsheet tips from issues of *PC World* magazine and frequently asked questions.

4. At http://www.finance-analyst.com there is a monthly newsletter with spreadsheet tips and hints.

5. At Alan's Excel Goodies (http://www.barasch.com/excel/) there is

information on Excel Visual Basic for Applications with code examples, frequently asked questions and Excel links.

6. Free answers to your questions on Excel are offered by
http://www.allexperts.com/getExpert.asp?Category=1059

■ 50. Changing the status bar and caption text

Try this macro.

```
Sub display()
Application.Caption = "LPX Mobile plc"
Application.DisplayStatusBar = True
Application.StatusBar = "Project by L.J.Smith ©2001"
End Sub
```

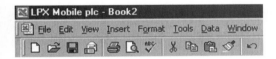

Appendix

Contents

- Excel glossary
- Excel toolbars
- Keyboard Shortcuts in Excel
- Error messages in Excel
- Taking screen shots
- Coursework requirements of the different examination boards

■ Excel Glossary

Absolute reference
An **absolute reference** is one that will not change if a formula is copied to a different cell. It is of the form **B7**.

Active cell
The **active cell** is the one that has been selected. It is shown with a thick black border.

Advanced filter
The **advanced filter** function is a filter that enables the user to search data based on complex criteria.

AutoFilter
The **AutoFilter** is a simple filter for selected records on simple criteria.

Auto_close
The **auto_close** macro is a macro that runs automatically when a file is closed.

Auto_open
The **auto_open** macro is a macro that runs automatically when a file is opened.

AutoSum
The **AutoSum** function is used to add the contents of chosen cells.

Button
A **button** or **command button** is a small rectangle on the screen. Click on the button to run a macro.

Chart
A **chart** is a graph in Microsoft Excel.

Check box
A **check box** is a small box on the screen that can either be selected or not selected. Clicking on a check box puts a little tick in the box. This is called **checking**. Clicking again to remove the tick is called **unchecking**.

Combo box
A **combo box** offers the user a choice. Clicking on the combo boxes displays the choices available in a list. One of these choices can be selected. It can also be called a drop-down box.

Comment
A **comment** is a way of adding extra information about a cell. The text appears on a small 'Post-it' note called the comment box.

Dialogue box
A **dialogue box** (or in American English a dialog box) is a box on the screen that enables the user to select choices and/or enter data.

Drop down box	See combo box
Formula	A **formula** is an equation that performs calculations on values in your worksheet. All formulas begin with =, e.g. ` = H4+H5 `
Formula bar	The **formula bar** is a box on the Excel screen, beneath the toolbars and above the column headings. The value of the selected cell or its formula appears in this box and can be edited here.
Front end	A **front end** is the name given to a user-friendly interface that appears on the screen when the file is loaded. Usually it will give the user a menu of options.
Function	A **function** is a built-in calculation in Excel, e.g. SUM, MAX, MIN and IF. A function is used in a formula, e.g. ` = SUM(H4:H5) `
Gridlines	The **gridlines** are (usually grey) lines dividing up the cells. You can choose whether or not to display and print the gridlines.
Legend	The **legend** is the key on an Excel chart.
List box	A **list box** is similar to a combo box; a list box displays the choices available in a list format. The user can scroll down to see additional choices.
Lookup	**Lookup** is an Excel function that looks up values in a table.
Macro	A **macro** is a program that stores a series of Microsoft Excel commands so that they can be executed as a single command. Macros can be recorded or written in Microsoft Visual Basic. Macros automate complex tasks and so save time by reducing the number of steps required to carry out a common task.
Message box	A **message box** is a small box on the screen, usually to give the user some information.
Named cells	It is possible to give a cell or a range of cells a name. This makes it easier to refer to these cells.
Nested IF	Including one or more IF statements inside another IF statement to give more than two choices.
Option button	An **option button** is used for choosing **one** from a list of options. You can select only one option button at a time. Also called a radio button.
Relative reference	A **relative reference** in a formula stores the position of a cell relative to the cell that contains the formula. When copied it will change depending on the cell it is copied to. It is of the form **B7**.
Scenario	A **scenario** is a set of values that are saved in a worksheet. Several different groups of values can be created and saved.
Scroll bar	The **vertical scroll bar** appears on the right hand side of the screen, to enable the user to move up and down a worksheet. The **horizontal scroll bar** at the bottom right of the screen, enables the user to move to the right or left in a worksheet. It is possible to add your own scroll bar, linked to a cell, to increase or decrease the value in the cell.
Spinner	A **spinner** consists of two arrows on the screen; one pointing up, the other down. Clicking on the up arrow increases a value in a cell, clicking the down arrow decreases it.
Start-up folder	Whenever Microsoft Excel is loaded, any files in this folder will be opened automatically.

Status bar   A horizontal bar near the bottom of the screen that displays useful information about a selected command or an operation in progress, e.g. the status bar shows whether CAPS LOCK has been pressed or if you are recording a macro.

Tabs   The names of the different worksheets in a workbook appear on **tabs** at the bottom of the screen. To move to another worksheet, click on the tab.

Template   A **template** is a special sort of workbook that is used as the basis for other workbooks.
                        An Excel template is stored in the form *.xlt

Text wrap   Fitting text on to multiple lines so that it fits in one cell

Toolbar   A **toolbar** is a row of icons, usually but not always at the top of the screen. Additional toolbars can be added to suit the user.

UserForm   A **UserForm** is a dialogue box that enables you to run macros, perform other operations and enter data. It could be used as part of an automated front end.

Visual Basic   **Microsoft Visual Basic** is Microsoft Excel's own programming language. Macros are recorded or written and are stored in this language.

Workbook   A **workbook** is a standard Microsoft Excel file.
                        Workbook can contain many **worksheets**, so that related information can be stored on different worksheets in a single file.
                        A workbook is stored in the form *.xls

Worksheet   **Worksheets** are the main feature of Microsoft Excel. They are the documents used to store and work with data. They consist of a grid of cells in rows and columns.
                        They are also called a **spreadsheet** or just a **sheet**.
                        A worksheet is part of a **workbook**.

Excel toolbars

The Excel toolbars that you are most likely to use are shown below:

Standard toolbar

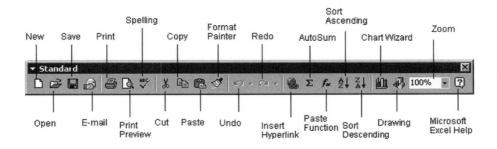

Formatting toolbar

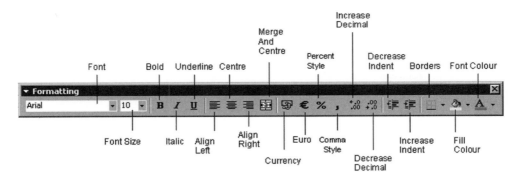

Drawing toolbar

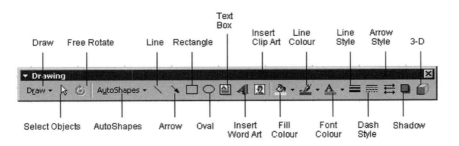

Picture toolbar

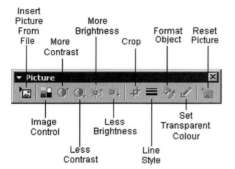

Insert Picture From File
More Contrast
More Brightness
Crop
Format Object
Reset Picture

Image Control
Less Brightness
Less Contrast
Line Style
Set Transparent Colour

Pivot table

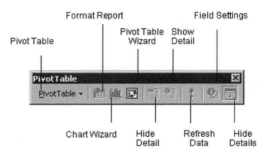

Format Report
Pivot Table
Pivot Table Wizard
Show Detail
Field Settings

Chart Wizard
Hide Detail
Refresh Data
Hide Details

Forms

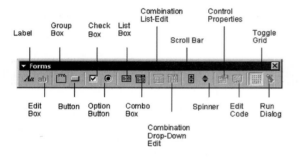

Label
Group Box
Check Box
List Box
Combination List-Edit
Scroll Bar
Control Properties
Toggle Grid

Edit Box
Button
Option Button
Combo Box
Combination Drop-Down Edit
Spinner
Edit Code
Run Dialog

Chart

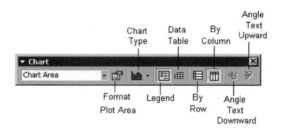

Chart Type
Data Table
By Column
Angle Text Upward

Format Plot Area
Legend
By Row
Angle Text Downward

Visual Basic

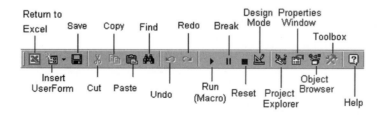

Return to Excel
Save
Copy
Find
Redo
Break
Design Mode
Properties Window
Toolbox

Insert UserForm
Cut
Paste
Undo
Run (Macro)
Reset
Project Explorer
Object Browser
Help

■ Keyboard shortcuts in Excel

There are several keyboard shortcuts to help you move around the screen in Excel and perform other common tasks. Here are some of the most useful.

Keystroke	Action
HOME	Changes active cell to column A in the same row
CTRL + HOME	Changes active cell to A1
CTRL + END	Changes active cell to the bottom right of all cells used
PAGE DOWN	Moves down one page
PAGE UP	Moves up one page
ALT + PAGE DOWN	Moves right one page
ALT + PAGE UP	Moves left one page
CTRL + PAGE DOWN	Moves to the next worksheet
CTRL + PAGE UP	Moves to the previous worksheet
F3	Pastes a name (of a range of cells) into a formula
F4	Repeats last action
F5	Go to. Then type in the cell required, e.g. H6
SHIFT + ENTER	Enters data and moves up one row
SHIFT + F2	Inserts a comment
SHIFT + F5	Find
SHIFT + F11	Inserts a new worksheet
SHIFT + SPACEBAR	Selects current row
CTRL + SPACEBAR	Selects current column
CTRL + A	Selects entire worksheet
CTRL + 1	Format cells
CTRL + 7	Toggle standard toolbar on and off
CTRL + Z	Undo
CTRL + X	Cut
CTRL + C	Copy
CTRL + V	Paste

CTRL + K	Insert a hyperlink
CTRL + F9	Minimise current window
CTRL + F10	Maximise current window
ALT + F1	Draw graph of selected cells
ALT + F8	Run a macro
ALT + F11	Load Visual Basic Editor
ALT + =	AutoSum. (The same as clicking the AutoSum icon)
ALT + '	Displays the Style format
ALT + ENTER	Adds another line to the cell
CTRL + ;	Enter current date
CTRL + :	Enter current time
CTRL + ` (next to 1 on keyboard)	Toggle between displaying values and displaying formulas
CTRL + SHIFT + _	Remove all borders
CTRL + SHIFT + O	Select all cells with comments

■ Error Messages in Excel

Error message	What it means
#####	The column is not wide enough to display the number stored. Make your column wider.
#VALUE!	A cell contains text when it is expected to contain a number. This cell is probably in a formula that cannot be calculated. Check the formula.
#DIV/0!	A formula involves division by zero or a blank cell. Check the formula.
#NAME?	The formula refers to a named range of cells that does not exist. Check the formula.
#N/A	A formula refers to a cell that does not contain the required information, for example in a LOOKUP. Check the formula.
#REF!	This occurs when a cell reference in a formula is not valid. Possibly caused by reference to a cell that has been deleted.
#NUM!	A problem has occurred with a number in a formula, for example the number may be too large or too small.
#NULL!	A formula refers to an incorrect cell reference. Probably caused by typing errors in entering the reference.

Taking screen shots

Screen shots of your system in action are vital both to prove that the system is working properly and to include in the user guide and technical instructions.

Using Windows Paint

To get a screen shot in Windows, press the **Print Screen** key on the keyboard. This puts the whole screen into the Windows clipboard.

You can then use **Edit, Paste** to paste the screen shot into your work.

The steps are:

1. Press the **Print Screen** key to capture the screen shot.

2. Switch to **Windows Paint**.

3. Click on **Edit, Paste**.

4. You may be told your image is too big and asked if you would like to expand the image. Click on **Yes**.

5. Save the image. (In *Windows 98* or later, you can save the image as a much smaller file by saving it as a **jpg** or a **gif**.).

6. Insert this image in your document.

If you only need to display part of a screen shot you will need to **crop** it. Cropping means cutting unwanted parts from the top, bottom or sides of a picture. Cropped pictures are smaller and so use less disk space.

Using Paint Shop Pro

Image manipulation software like Paint Shop Pro is ideal for screen shots, offering different options such as easy cropping and reducing to 16 or 256 colours to reduce the file size.

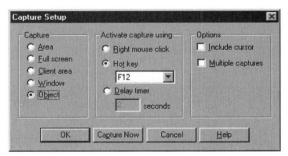

In Paint Shop Pro, the first step is to set up how the Screen will operate.

1. Click on **Capture, Setup**. Paint Shop Pro will open the **Capture Setup Dialog Box** shown below.

2. Click on the required **Capture** type.

The capture type determines which area of the screen will be copied.

Area	Select a rectangular portion of the screen
Full Screen	Copy the entire screen
Client Area	Copy the input area of the active window
Window	Copy the entire active window
Object	Copy a window feature or group of features

3. Click on the way you want the screen capture to operate.

Captures can be activated by using the right mouse button, setting up a Hot Key or setting a timer delay.

There is an option to include the cursor or not. If you choose to include the cursor make sure it is in the correct position before activating the capture.

4. Click on the **OK** Button to close the dialog box and save the capture set-up settings.

To activate the screen capture choose **Capture now** from the Capture Setup box or Start from the capture menu, or press the hot key.

■ Coursework specifications

■ Introduction

The following section offers guidance on these issues:

➤ Structure of the new AS and A2 qualifications.

➤ Pointers to the examination board modules/units supported in this book.

➤ Assessment criteria currently used by the different examination boards.

■ Course structure

All three examining boards, AQA, OCR and Edexcel, offer Advanced Subsidiary (AS) and Advanced (A) Level qualifications in Information and Communications Technology (ICT). The AS level is a qualification in its own right or can be the first half of the A level. With all the boards, the AS course consists of three units; two are examined by written papers and the third unit is a coursework submission. The full A level is made up of the AS units plus three more units called A2. The first two A2 units are again examined by written papers and the third unit is again coursework. The information in this book can be used to support the following coursework units where you are required to provide an ICT solution based on the use of **appropriate applications software.**

☐ AQA

■ MODULE 3 (AS)

This module counts for 40% of the AS level mark and 20% of the A level mark. You are expected to tackle a task-related problem using the facilities of one piece of **generic software**.

■ MODULE 6 (A2)

You are required to research a realistic problem for which there must be a *real end-user*. The solution may be provided by **generic application software**

This module is 20% of the A level mark.

OCR

■ UNIT 2513 (AS)

This unit consists of structured practical ICT tasks set by the board. You are required to base a solution on the use of an **appropriate applications package.** This unit of assessment counts for 40% of the AS level mark and 20% of the A level mark.

■ UNIT 2516 (A2)

This unit requires you to identify a well-defined problem, involving a third-party user and to generate a solution using **applications software** as chosen by yourself. This module is 20% of the A level mark.

Edexcel

Unit 3 (AS) consists of two coursework tasks worth 40% of the AS assessment.

Task 1 (16%) ✘ is a written report/study of an ICT administration process.

Task 2 (24%) ✓ requires you to produce and document an ICT solution to a significant problem using a standard **commercial application generator**

Unit 6 (A2) consists of two coursework tasks worth 40% of the A2 assessment.

Task 3 ✘ is a written report on ICT issues.

Task 4 ✘ requires you to produce and document an ICT solution using event-driven object-based programming.

■ Assessment criteria

AQA AS Module 3

The project is marked out of a total of 60.

Specification	13 marks
Implementation	20 marks
User Testing	12 marks
Evaluation	6 marks
User Documentation	9 marks
TOTAL	60 marks

Specification (13 marks)

11–13 You have:

- produced a detailed requirements specification for the identified problem, matching end-user(s) stated needs
- clearly stated the input, processing and output needs, which match the requirements specification
- completed effective designs to enable independent third-party implementation of the solution
- determined an appropriate test strategy and devised an effective test and full testing plan; the testing plan includes the test data and expected outcomes and directly relates to the requirements specification

8–10 You have:

- produced a detailed requirements specification for the identified problem, matching end-user(s) stated needs
- stated the input, processing and output needs, which match the requirements specification
- completed designs though they lack detail and thus do not allow independent third-party implementation of the solution or are inefficient in relation to the problem stated
- determined a test strategy and devised testing plans but these are limited in scope and do not relate to the requirements specification stated

4–7 You have:

- produced a requirements specification for the identified problem, although it does not fully match end-user(s) stated needs or lacks detail and clarity
- stated the input, processing and output needs, although these do not fully match the requirements' specification or are not sufficiently clear
- attempted design work although this is incomplete and does not reflect an efficient solution to the problem stated
- determined a test strategy although this is either incomplete or does not relate to the requirements specification stated; the testing plan is either vague or missing

1–3
- The requirements specification is vague or missing
- The input, processing and output needs are only vaguely considered or are absent
- There is little or no design effort
- The test strategy and testing plans are vague or missing

0 You have produced no work

Implementation (20 marks)

16–20 You have:

- developed an effective solution operable in the proposed environment by the intended end-user
- used appropriate data capture and validation procedures, data organisation methods, output contents and formats and user interface(s)
- fully employed generic and package specific skills in an effective and appropriate manner
- fully justified the selection of hardware and software facilities in relation to your designed solution designed

11–15 You have:

- developed a solution which is operable in the proposed environment by the intended end-user although it has some inefficiencies
- produced evidence of the use of appropriate data capture and validation procedures, data organisation methods, output contents and formats and user interface(s)
- fully employed generic and package specific skills but not always in an effective and appropriate manner
- justified the selection of some of the chosen hardware and software facilities in relation to the solution developed

6–10 You have:

- developed a partial solution, but those aspects completed are useable by the intended end-user
- produced evidence of the issue of some data capture and validation procedures, data organisation methods, output contents and formats and user interface(s)
- employed generic and package specific skills but not always in an effective and appropriate manner
- only vaguely justified the selection of some of the chosen hardware and software facilities in relation to the solution developed

1–5 You have:

- developed a very limited solution which is not practically operable in the proposed environment by the intended end-user
- used few, if any, data capture and validation procedures, data organisation methods, output contents and formats and user interface(s)
- used the generic and package specific skills in a simplistic way and/or not always applied them appropriately
- not justified the selection of chosen hardware and software facilities in relation to the solution developed

0 You have not implemented the system

Testing (12 marks)

9–12 You have:

- followed the devised test strategy and test plan in a systematic manner using typical, erroneous and extreme (boundary) data
- fully documented the results of testing with outputs cross-referenced to the original plan
- clearly documented corrective action taken due to test results

5–8 You have:

- followed the test strategy and devised plan in a systematic manner but using only normal data
- partially documented the results of testing with some evidence of outputs cross-referenced to the original plan
- produced some evidence of corrective action taken due to test results

1–4 You have:

- followed the test strategy and devised plan in a limited manner using only normal data
- produced little or no documentation of the results of testing
- given little or no indication of corrective action required due to test results

0 There is no evidence of testing

Evaluation (6 marks)

4–6 You have:

- fully assessed the effectiveness of the solution by meeting the detailed requirements specification and shown full awareness of the criteria for a successful information technology solution
- clearly identified the limitations of the system

1–3 You have:

- partly assessed the effectiveness of the solution in meeting the original requirements specification and shown only partial awareness of the criteria for a successful information technology solution
- been vague about, or failed to mention, the limitations of the solution

0 There is no evidence of evaluation

User documentation (9 marks)

7–9 There is extensive user documentation for the solution which covers all relevant aspects including normal operation and common problems and is appropriate to the needs of the end-user

4–6 A user guide is present which describes the functionality of the solution and is appropriate to the needs of the end-user

1–3 A limited user guide is present which describes only the basic functionality of the solution

0 There is no evidence of user documentation

AQA A2 Module 6

The project is marked out of a total of 90.

Analysis	18 marks
Design	16 marks
Implementation	15 marks
Testing	15 marks
User Guide	8 marks
Evaluation	10 marks
Report	8 marks
Total	90 marks

Analysis (18 marks)

15–18 You have:

- identified an appropriate problem in conjunction with your end-user and independently of the teacher
- provided a clear, statement covering both the context and the nature of the problem
- clearly identified and delimited a substantial and realistic problem, and recognised the requirements of intended user(s) and the capabilities and limitations of the resources available
- specified and clearly documented all the requirements
- fully identified the information flow and data dynamics of the problem
- indicated in your analysis an appreciation of the full potential of the appropriate hardware and software facilities available and also, if appropriate, their limitations
- identified the user's current IT skill level and training needs
- identified qualitative and quantitative evaluation criteria in details and completed your analysis without undue assistance

10–14 You have:

- identified an appropriate problem with reference to your end-user and independently of the teacher
- provided a clear outline statement covering both the context and the nature of the problem
- identified a substantial problem and recognised many of the requirements of intended users and many of the capabilities and limitations of the resources available
- provided documentation which is intelligible but lacking in some respects

10–13   You have:

- indicated in your analysis which software will be used but it may not be obvious how the software will be used
- partly identified the information flow and data dynamics of the problem
- identified reasonable evaluation criteria
- required some assistance to reach this stage
- alternatively, identified a relatively straightforward problem and proceeded unaided, covering most or all of the points required for 15–18 marks

6–9   You have:

- needed some guidance from the teacher to identify an appropriate problem with an end-user
- provided a simple outline statement
- selected a substantial problem and attempted to identify many of the requirements of intended users and many of the capabilities and limitations of the resources available but needed assistance in analysing the problem
- identified only a limited subset of the information flow and data dynamics of the problem
- provided documentation but it is incomplete
- alternatively, identified a fairly simple problem and recognised most of the requirements of intended users and most of the capabilities and limitations of the resources available
- needed assistance in analysing the problem; with documentation that is complete in most respects

3–5   You have:

- required considerable guidance from the teacher to identify an appropriate problem with an end-user
- provided a superficial outline statement
- identified a fairly simple problem and recognised some of the requirements of intended users and some of the capabilities and limitations of the resources available
- provided few, if any, indications of what must be done to carry out the task
- given little indication of how the software will be used
- not identified the information flow and data dynamics of the problem
- provided weak and incomplete documentation
- needed much assistance in analysing the problem

1–2   You have:

- identified a simple problem or been given a straightforward problem
- given only minimal recognition of either the requirements of intended users or capabilities and limitations of the resources available
- provided poor documentation and needed substantial assistance

0   No analysis is present

Design

GENERATION OF POSSIBLE SOLUTIONS AND SOLUTION DESIGN

The design phase includes bringing together the results of the analysis and gathering and ordering information related to the background of the problem into the generation of a range of possible solutions which meet them. This may be alternative types of package or alternative solutions within a package. The solution design should be specified so that a competent person can implement it. There should be a clear specification of how each of the sub-tasks identified in the analysis is to be solved.

The detailed design (16 marks)

13–16 You have:

- considered a relevant range of appropriate approaches to a solution in detail, given compelling reasons for final choice of solution which have been fully justified, and fully considered likely effectiveness
- specified a completely detailed solution which a competent third party could carry out, clearly breaking down the proposed solution into sub-tasks with necessary indications of how these are to be solved, and specified and clearly documented all the requirements
- included a well-defined schedule and work plan, showing in detail how the task is to be carried out and what is required in a comprehensible manner; this can include layout sheets, record structures, spreadsheet plans, design for data-capture sheets etc. as appropriate
- devised an effective and full testing plan with a comprehensive selection of test data and reasons for the choice of the data clearly specified
- completed this stage without assistance

9–12 You have:

- considered a relevant range of appropriate approaches to a solution, giving reasons for your final choice of solution and reasonably considering likely effectiveness
- specified a solution so that a competent third party could carry it out but with some difficulty, and breaking down the proposed solution into sub-tasks with some indication of how these are to be solved, specifying and clearly documenting some of the requirements
- included a schedule and work plan showing how the tasks are to be carried out, showing what is required in a reasonable manner; this can include layout sheets, record structures, spreadsheet plans, design for data-capture sheets etc. as appropriate
- devised a testing plan with some tests clearly specified
- completed this stage without undue assistance

6–8 You have:

- provided a limited range of approaches which may have required some assistance; the reasons given for the final choice are weak and likely effectiveness has not been discussed in detail
- given sufficient detail so that you, but not another person, can replicate the solution at a later date; an attempt has been made to break down the solution into sub-tasks with some indications of how these are to be solved; the documentation is clear but lacking in some respects
- provided a schedule and work plan but these are limited
- presented a testing plan
- completed this without undue assistance

3–5 You have:

- considered only one approach which may have required considerable assistance, giving only vague reasons for the formal choice and without discussing likely effectiveness
- given sufficient detail so that the candidate, but not another person, can replicate the solution at a later date but with some difficulty; an attempt has been made to break down the solution into sub-tasks but with insufficient indications of how these are to be solved; the documentation is lacking in many respects
- provided a schedule and work plan but these are poorly thought out
- supplied a poor testing plan
- required possibly substantial assistance

1–2 You have:

- given little or no consideration to approaches to the solution and no or invalid reasons for final choice of solution
- chosen a superficial outline of the solution so that you are unable to replicate the solution at a later date; little attempt has been made to break down the problem into sub-tasks; schedule and work plan are vague or missing; testing plan is vague or missing; documentation is poor and substantial assistance may have been required

0 No detail of chosen solution given

Implementation (15 marks)

11–15 You have fully implemented the detailed design unaided, in an efficient manner with no obvious defects, fully exploiting all the appropriate facilities of the software and hardware available; documentation is clear and thorough

6–10 You have:

- implemented the essential elements of the design reasonably effectively and largely unaided; implementation has exploited some of the relevant features of the software and hardware available; documentation lacks detail or may be missing completely
- alternatively, fully implemented a simple design

1–5   You have only partially implemented the design; the implementation has exploited few of the relevant features of the software and hardware available; the documentation lacks detail or may be missing completely

0   There is no implementation

Testing (15 marks)

11–15   You have shown insight in demonstrating effective test data to cover most or all eventualities and provided clear evidence of full end-user involvement in testing. The system works with a full range of test data (typical, extreme, erroneous); the test outputs are annotated fully

6–10   You have demonstrated a range of appropriate test data perhaps with some assistance and some evidence of end-user involvement during testing. The system works with a limited range of test data; the tests outputs are annotated to a limited extent

1–5   There is little evidence of testing and only limited involvement of the end-user in testing. It does not meet the design specification

0   There is no evidence of testing

User guide (8 marks)

6–8   You have produced a comprehensive, well illustrated user guide that deals with all aspects of the system (installation, backup procedures, general use and troubleshooting)

4–5   You have produced an illustrated user guide that deals with general use of the system but only vaguely considers the other areas required for 6–8 marks

1–3   A user guide is produced that deals with general use of the system

0   No user guide is present

Evaluation of the project (10 marks)

9–10   You have considered clearly a full range of qualitative and quantitative criteria for evaluating the solution, fully evaluated your solution intelligently against user requirements, and provided evidence of end-user involvement during this stage

6–8   You have discussed a range of relevant criteria for evaluating the solution, evaluated your solution against user requirements in most respects, identified some, but not all, performance indicators, and specified any modifications to meet possible major limitations and/or enhancements, maybe with assistance

3–5   You have only partially evaluated the system against the original specification and user requirements. This may be because the original specification was poor. Few, if any, performance indicators have been identified. Discussion concerning the limitations or enhancements to the system are largely absent or have required some prompting

1–2   You have made little attempt at evaluation. No performance indicators have been identified. Discussion concerning the limitations or enhancements to the system are absent or limited and have required considerable prompting

0   No attempt at evaluation has been made

Preparation of the report (8 marks)

7–8   You have produced a well-written, fully illustrated, organised report, describing the project accurately and concisely

5–6   You have produced a well-written report but it lacks good organisation. Alternatively the report is well-organised but of limited quality

3–4   Your report is of generally poor quality but shows evidence of organisation. There are deficiencies and omissions

1–2   Your report is poorly organised and presented with few or no diagrams. There are a considerable number of omissions

0   No report is present

OCR Module 2516

The project is marked out of a total of 120.

Definition and Analysis	25 marks
Design	21 marks
Development, testing and implementation	35 marks
Documentation	24 marks
Evaluation	15 marks

(a) Definition, investigation and analysis (25 marks)

i. Definition – nature of the problem solved (5 marks)   You should not expect the examiner to be familiar with the theory and practice in the area of the chosen system. You should give a brief description of the organisation (e.g. firm or business) involved and the current methods used in the chosen areas that may form the basis of the project, and a clear statement of the origins and form of data. At this stage the exact scope of the project may not be known and it may lead to an interview with the user.

1. A vague description of the organisation
2. Some description of both the stages of study and organisation involved
3. A good description of either the area or organisation with some description of the other.
4. A clear description with one element missing (for example, origins of the data).
5. An excellent description with all elements present

ii. Investigation and analysis (20 marks)

This section is the 'systems analysis'. The question is not how a system performs detailed tasks, but rather how the project progresses from the original data to the results. You should describe how user requirements were ascertained (possibly by long discussions with users; question and answer sessions should be recorded and outcomes agreed). A clear requirements specification should be defined. Alternative outline solutions should be discussed and evaluated against one another

16–20

Excellent user involvement with detailed recording of the user's requirements. Alternative approaches have been discussed in depth. All other items must be present, showing a thorough analysis of the system to be computerised. A detailed requirements specification has been produced

11–15

Good user involvement and recording of the interview(s). Most of the necessary items have been covered including a detailed discussion or alternative approaches. However, one or two items have been omitted. A requirements specification is present but with some omissions

6–10

Some evidence that an attempt has been made to interview the user and some recording of it has been made. Attempts at some of the other items have been made. An attempt has been made to develop a requirements specification

1–5

Some elements have been discussed but little or no user involvement

(b) Design (21 marks)

i. Nature of the solution (13 marks)

A detailed systems design (including diagrams as appropriate), should be produced and agreed with users. Proposed data structures should be described and design limitations included. Design of the user interface is of paramount importance and should be documented in detail in the form of data capture forms, input formats (with examples of screen layouts if necessary), and output formats should be included where relevant. A detailed summary of the aims and objectives should also be included. These are the design specifications which should be agreed with the user

11–13

A clear set of objectives with a detailed and complete design specification, which is logically correct. There are also detailed written descriptions of any processes/modules and a clear, complete definition of any data structures. The specification is sufficient for someone to pick up and develop an end result using the software and hardware specified in the requirements specification

6–10

A clear set of objectives have been defined; a full design specification is included but there may be some errors or logical inconsistencies, e.g. validation specified may be inadequate or field lengths incorrect

3–6	The major objective of the new system has been adequately summarised, but omissions have been made. There is a brief outline of a design specification, including mock-ups of inputs and outputs, task model described (including any diagrams). However, there is a lack of completeness with omissions from the task model, inputs and outputs. Data structures have been identified but there may be inadequate detail
1–2	Some vague discussion of what the system will do with brief diagrammatic representation of the new system

ii. Intended benefits (3 marks)	There should be some discussion of the relative merits of the intended system and of the previous mode of operation. This may include any degree of generality beyond the original scope of the system. One mark should be awarded for each valid benefit up to a maximum of three marks

iii. Limits of scope of situation (5 marks)	This may include volume (sizing limitations), limitations imposed by the interface and/or limitations of the facilities used. For full marks there must be some estimate of the size of storage space required for the implemented system.
4–5	A detailed description of the system limitations has been given, including the estimate of the size of the files required for the implemented system
2–3	The major limitations of the system have been adequately summarised, but omissions have been made
1	A vague discussion of what the system limitations are

(c) Software development, testing and implementation (35 marks)

i. Software development and testing (18 marks)	A technical description of how the solution relates to the design specification produced and agreed with the user should be included. It is your responsibility to produce evidence of your development work and for producing a test plan for the system. It is vital to produce test cases and to show that they work. To do this, it is necessary not only to have test data, but to know what the expected results are with that data
	An attempt should be made to show that all parts of the system have been tested, including those sections dealing with unexpected or invalid data as well as extreme cases. Showing that many other cases of test data are likely to work – by including the outputs that they produce – is another important feature. Evidence of testing is essential. Comments by teachers and others are of value, but the test plan must be supported by evidence in the report of a properly designed testing process. The examiner must be left in no doubt the system actually works in the target environment. This evidence may be in the form of a hardcopy output (possibly including screen dumps), photographs or VHS video

14–18	Technical evidence is provided in the form of printouts. Data structures are illustrated as part of the listings where appropriate, detailing their purpose. There is a full set of printouts showing input and output as well as data structures. All hardcopy evidence is fully annotated and cross-referenced. A full test plan, with evidence of each test run is present in the report, together with the expected output. The test plan should cover as many different paths through the system as is feasible, including valid, invalid and extreme cases. Marks may be lost for lack of evidence of a particular test run or lack of expected results
9–13	Evidence of tailored software packages/tailored interface software/tailored client software are provided in the form of printouts. Data structures are illustrated as part of the listings where appropriate, detailing their purposes. There is some annotation evident to illustrate how the package was tailored for a particular purpose or to indicate the purpose of sections of code in a program listing. The developed solution partially fulfils the design specification. There should be at least eight test runs together with a test plan and hardcopy evidence. However, the test plan has omissions in it and/or not all the cases have been tested (i.e. have no evidence of testing)
5–8	Evidence of tailored software packages/tailored interface software/tailored client software etc. are provided in the form of printouts. Data structures are illustrated as annotation evident to illustrate how the package was tailored for a particular purpose or to indicate the purpose of sections of code in a program listing. The developed solution has logical flaws and does not fulfil the design specification. There is little evidence of testing with a badly developed test plan with clear omissions. There is no description of the relationship between the structure of the development work and the testing in evidence
1–4	Evidence of tailoring of a software package or integration of interface software is tailored into a system and is provided in the form of printouts but with no annotation or relationship to a test plan or test run. The developed solution does not fulfil the design specification. A collection of hardcopy test run outputs with no test plan, or a test plan with no hardcopy evidence may also be present. A teacher may award up to 2 marks if they have shown the system working satisfactorily and there is no hard evidence in the project report
ii. Implementation (10 marks)	It is recognised that the user organisation (preferably 'third party'), may not fully implement the system, although this is the ultimate aim. However, to score any marks in this section there must be some evidence that the person for whom the system was written has seen the system in operation. This can be done in a number of ways: such as by inviting the user to see the product and by your ability to demonstrate the system, or by taking the system to the user involved. There should be an implementation plan written, including details of system changeover, training required and details of user testing
8–10	A clear and detailed implementation plan, including detailed stages of user testing. All aspects of user testing, user acceptance, implementation and system changeover have been documented. There is written evidence available from the user that the system has been fully tested

5–7	A good implementation plan with details of training required. There is written evidence available from the third party user indicating that they have seen the system in operation
1–3	Details of system changeover have been documented with some recognition that the user(s) will require training. Some evidence of user testing is given, usually by questionnaire or written comments by fellow students or others who were not directly involved in the development of the system
0	No evidence that the third party user has used the system. No written implementation plan

iii. Appropriateness of structure and exploitation of available facilities (7 marks)	Some discussion of the suitability of methods and any product (e.g. hardware or software) used for the particular system should be included. Some recognition and discussion of the problems encountered and actions taken when appropriate should also be included. A log of such problems should be kept. Suitability for subsequent maintainability and extendibility.
4–7	A complete discussion of the hardware and software available and how they were suitable in solving the given problem, together with a good, informative explanation of the problems encountered and how they were overcome
1–3	Some attempt at discussing either the suitability of the hardware and software or the problems encountered

(d) Documentation (24 marks)

i. Technical (10 marks)	Much of the documentation will have been produced as a by-product of design and development work and as a part of writing up the report to date. However, a technical guide is a standalone document produced to facilitate easy maintenance and upgrade of a system. The contents of the guide should, where relevant, include the following: data structures used and/or database modelling and organisation including relationships, screens, reports and menus; data dictionary, where appropriate; data flow (or navigation paths through the interface); annotated software details in the form of printouts; detailed flowcharts/transition diagrams as necessary; details of any functions, procedures, macros etc. and any formulae used. All parts of the guide should be fully annotated since this is very important for subsequent development of the system. The specifications of the hardware and software on which the system can be implemented should be included
	Since the system in the technical guide will differ from one project to another, professional judgement as to what would be necessary for another analyst to maintain and develop the system has to be made.
7–10	No major omissions, with all parts fully annotated. Marks will be lost for inadequate items of documentation, e.g. non-specification of hardware on which the system can be implemented. For full marks the guide should be well presented rather than just a collection of items

| 3–6 | One or two major omissions, but the rest is fully annotated |
| 1–2 | Some items are present but little annotation |

ii. User (14 marks)

Clear guidance, as friendly as possible, should be given to the user for all operations that they would be required to perform. These would include input format with screen display's, print options, back-ups (file integrity routines), security of access to data and a guide to common errors which may occur. (Note: you will not be required to copy out large volumes of any underlying software's user-guide, but to produce a non-technical and easy-to-follow guide for someone with little computer knowledge.) Some mention here of the relationship between items of software and the data they deal with may be relevant. The user guide should be well-presented with an index and, where necessary, a glossary of the terms used. Alternatively, an electronic guide could be based around hypertext links (screen dumps will be required)

10–14	A full user guide with all options described, well presented (possibly as booklet), with an index and a glossary. No omission of any of the options available (including backup outlines, guide to common errors). Marks may be lost for inadequate descriptions of some options. For full marks, good on-screen help should exist
5–9	All but one or two options fully described, e.g. back-up routines not mentioned. In the main the options are easy for the user to follow with screen displays
1–2	An incomplete, badly produced guide. No screen displays/interface mock-ups. Some options briefly described but difficult for the user to follow

(e) Evaluation (15 marks)

i. Discussion of the degree of success in meeting the original objectives (6 marks)

This discussion should demonstrate your ability to evaluate the effectiveness of the completed system. The original objectives stated in requirements specification should be matched with achievements, taking into account the limitations. User evaluation is also essential and should arise from a questionnaire or, preferably, direct user evaluation. For full marks it is important that the user provides sets of data as they are likely to occur in practice, and that the results arising from such data be given. This data is typical data rather than test data and it may show up faults or problems that your own test data failed to find

4–6	A full discussion, taking each objective mentioned in (b) (i) and explaining the degree of success in meeting them, indicating where in the project evidence can be found to support this or reasons why they were not met
1–3	Some discussion about a number of objectives, but some omissions or inadequate explanation of success or failure
0	No discussion present

ii. Evaluate the user's response to the system (5 marks)

It is important that the user is not assumed to be an expert in computer jargon, so some effort must be made to ensure that the system is user-friendly. It will be assumed that the user will have considerable knowledge of the underlying theory of the business being computerised. Clarity of menus, clear on-screen help and easy methods of inputting data are all examples of how the system can be made more user-friendly. Here marks are awarded for the degree of satisfaction that the user indicates in the acceptance procedure. Could the system, or its results, be used? Was the system specification achieved? Do any system faults still exist? You should evaluate users' response to the final version of the system

4–5   A fully user-friendly system has been produced. The user indicates that the system fully meets the specification given in section (a), and there are no known faults with the system

2–3   The system is, in the main, user-friendly, but there is room for improvement (e.g. no on-screen help has been provided). The user indicates that the system could be used but there are some faults, which need to be rectified

1   Some effort has been made to make the system user-friendly, but the user still has difficulty using the system

(iii) Desirable extensions (4 marks)   As a result of completing the system, you have identified the good and bad points of the final system highlighting limitations and necessary extensions to the system, indicating how the extensions could be carried out. You have:

4   1. clearly portrayed the good and bad points of the system indicating the imitations, possible extensions and how to carry out the extensions

3   2. clearly identified good and bad points of the system, limitations and the possible extensions;

2   3. clearly identified good and bad points and any limitations;

1   4. identified the obvious good points of the system, and possibly some bad points or limitations

Edexcel

Edexcel Task 2 will consist of a practical, documented ICT solution to a significant problem that focuses on one of the areas of:

- modelling
- communications
- modern user interface
- multimedia
- data logging involving significant file processing
- manipulation.

It is expected that such a task will involve the advanced use of one or more commercial/ industrial standard application generators. **In general, it will not be expected for you to employ programming skills**. You will want to use the best software to which you have access in a manner that is most appropriate to the task in hand. Thus it is the intention that the following marking guidelines could be applied in most situations. You will be expected to produce documented evidence under the specified ten sections.

Marking of Task 2

The assessment guidance gives three mark ranges to correspond to what may be considered as a foundation task (F), an intermediate task (I) and a higher task (H). The teacher examiner will have to exercise judgment as to what level of task the student has attempted.

Section	Assessment Criteria	Mark Ranges		
		F	**I**	**H**
Specification	Clear description of the task to be attempted. Particular references to the potential users and the type of processing that will be required. Statements that justify an ICT approach to the task and some consideration as to possible wider implications.	0-3	3-6	6-9
Facilities	Discussion of the suitability of specific hardware and software required as they relate to the demands of the task in hand.	0-1	1-2	2-3
Analysis	Evidence that a thorough investigation of the background to the task has taken place in relationship to the potential users of the product. This should include, where appropriate, an analysis of any existing systems that are to be replaced and indications of from where the evidence has been gathered. Description of the complete data requirements of the proposed system and indications of the sources of these data.	0-3	3-6	6-9
Design	Top view of the proposed system showing the sources of the information, the information flow paths, the general nature of the processing required related to appropriate application generators and any remedial process that may be built in (data validation). Complete designs of all proposed input and output interfaces; for example: screen designs, report structures (of input signals if a real-time application). Complete designs of any required processing structures such as file structures, database structures, spreadsheet functions, hypertext connections, OLE sources and destinations.	0-3	3-6	6-9
Implementation	Detailed evidence of the implementation of the design. It is important that the relationship between the design and the implementation is clear, and this may include reporting any iteration between design and implementation that often takes place (prototyping). It could be an advantage to implement a system in a modular fashion and ensure that the documentation reflects this approach as it may assist in the awarding of deserved marks. Annotated hard copy should be produced where appropriate.	0-3	3-6	6-9

Section	Assessment Criteria	Mark Ranges		
		F	**I**	**H**
Testing	It is good practice to perform technical testing as integral with implementation. Nevertheless, to help you maximise credit for testing, it is sensible for you to give evidence, in a separate section, of what tests you they have designed and tried out. You should include evidence of results that show that the components of your implementation work as expected.	0-3	3-6	6-9
Documentation for the systems administrator	Documents that will assist a systems administrator install, test and troubleshoot the implemented system.	0-1	1-2	2-3
Documentation for the User	You will have to demonstrate that you appreciate what is likely to be understandable to a potential user. You should use suitable software to produce an attractive guide to your product.	0-1	1-2	2-3
User training needs	Statements concerning any prior knowledge and skills the user may require. A helpful walk-through example of using the system. A simple self-evaluation test for the user.	0-1	1-2	2-3
Evaluation	Reflective statements on how the final system meets the expectations of the specification with reference to reported reactions of users to the system.	0-1	1-2	2-3

Examining board qualifications

Full specifications for the qualifications are available at these web sites:

www.aqa.org.uk

www.ocr.org.uk

www.edexcel.org.uk

Index to *Spreadsheet* Projects